CONTENTS

The Purpose of This Series

Introduction

THE PURPOSE OF THIS SERIES

There are now over twenty books in this series, covering many areas of current thinking in education. A list of these will be found at the beginning of this book. These books are of interest to educators, trainers and administrators responsible for the implementation of educational policies in higher, further and continuing education. Each book contains extensive references to key works to enable the reader to pursue selected areas in more depth should he or she wish.

This is the second in a group of three books. The first, "Teaching, Learning and Communication", considers good communication between the teacher and learner as central to the education process. This book, the second, "Educating for a Computer Age" considers the role of the teacher in our changing society, looks at man´s present and future needs, distilling out guidelines for future action. The third book "Educational Futures", to be published shortly, explores the possibilities which arise as the full potential of the computer is realised and is used in education, and as more possibilities for education begin to exist outside the formal system.

P.J.Hills
Cambridge.

EDUCATING FOR A COMPUTER AGE

P.J. Hills

The present electronic revolution is reaching into every aspect
of our work, education and leisure. Across the world there
are initiatives to investigate this pervasive influence.
Developments in information technology will continue apace.
As increases in computer processing speeds and storage
capacities occur, a convergence of telecommunications and
computer networks will allow the development of national and
international networks of computer-based services. The computer will be used like the pocket calculator as a natural
extension of man's powers. This book shows how the computer can be used to enhance man's communication skills.
In exploring man's present and future needs and the education of generations to come, the book will be of wide interest
to educationalists and others concerned with the influence of
the computer on education and training. The emphasis
throughout is practical and an up-to-date picture of the current situation is given.

A volume in the CROOM HELM SERIES ON NEW
PATTERNS OF LEARNING
edited by P.J. Hills

NEW PATTERNS OF LEARNING SERIES
Edited by P.J. Hills, University of Cambridge

Educating for a Computer Age

PHILIP HILLS

CROOM HELM
London • New York • Sydney

© 1987 Philip Hills
Croom Helm Ltd, Provident House, Burrell Row,
Beckenham, Kent, BR3 1AT
Croom Helm Australia, 44-50 Waterloo Road,
North Ryde, 2113, New South Wales

British Library Cataloguing in Publication Data

Hills, P.J.
    Educating for a computer age.—(New
    patterns of learning series)
    1. Education — Data processing
    I. Title II. Series
    370'.28'5   LB1028.43

    ISBN 0-7099-4705-4

Published in the USA by
Croom Helm
in association with Methuen, Inc.
29 West 35th Street
New York, NY 10001

Library of Congress Cataloging-in-Publication Data

Hills, P.J. (Philip James)
    Educating for a computer age.

    (New patterns of learning series)
    Bibliography: p.
    Includes index.
    1. Education — data processing. 2. Computer-assisted
instruction. 3. Computer literacy. 4. Educational
technology. I. Title. II. Series.
LB1028.43.H55   1987   370'.285'4   86-32778
ISBN 0-7099-4705-4

Printed and bound in Great Britain by
Biddles Ltd, Guildford and King's Lynn

Introduction

This book is intended for educationalists, educators and teachers, define these as you will. Its message is a simple one:

> If teachers don't know where they are going they are liable to end up some place else.
>   (Adapted from Mager, 1962)

This book attempts to help them by outlining the educational scene as it is now and by providing some background and guidance for the situation that is to come. Teachers need to take positive action now, both to safeguard the education of present and future generations and to gain recognition of the importance of the teaching profession as guardians of our future.

There are many definitions of Information Technology, but the one which follows, generated in an educational context, is the one that has been borne in mind throughout the preparation of this book:

> Information Technology is the acquisition, production, transformation, storage and transmission of data by electronic means in forms such as vocal, pictorial, textual or numeric, such as to facilitate the interaction between people, and people and machines. It also includes applications and implications (social, economic and cultural) of these processes. (FEU, 1984)

Chapter 1 sets the scene for the electronic revolution in which we find ourselves. Chapter 2 examines in more detail the main agent of change in this revolution, the computer and allied developments in microelectronics and tele-communications. In Chapter 3 we look at the present educational scene, the aims of education, and present projects and initiatives in education.

Introduction

Chapters 4, 5 and 6 explore some of the internal functionings of man, his needs and his ability to process information, man in his surroundings, the tasks he is expected to perform and the ways in which he extends himself with the help of outside agencies. The computer as a potential "fourth brain" of man is introduced at this point as the ultimate extension of man. Chapter 7 considers the application of the computer and the methods of information technology to education.

Chapter 8 considers a possible role for the teacher in helping to plan for the future, and discusses why this is a role that he must accept. As computers begin to play more and more part in every aspect of our lives, because they are not only powerful tools in themselves but are capable of receiving and transmitting information anywhere in the world, questions, fears and doubts arise. Chapter 9 "The Computer: Master or Servant" explores these aspects.

The final chapter argues that the teaching profession is going through an identity crisis from which the teacher must emerge with the realisation that he is the person best placed to act both as a catalyst and disseminator of the seeds of positive action in our changing world.

Throughout the book I use the term "man", "he" etc. to denote both sexes. I have searched long and hard for an alternative and "(s)he" is the nearest I have come to a solution. As I find this cumbersome I have not used it. If anyone knows of a good solution to this problem I should be pleased to hear of it.

I have also used the terms "teacher" and "classroom" but this does not mean that I am concerned only with schools. It would be tedious to continually write "teachers and lecturers in schools, colleges, polytechnics and universities". The arguments which follow are in the main applicable to all levels of education. You are asked therefore to react to these aspects in the light of your own educational perspectives.

Introduction

I am indebted to many people who have helped in many
ways, through discussion, through contributing ideas
and through reading drafts of the text. I hope they
will forgive me for not mentioning them by name in
this introduction. Where I have quoted their work
their name is mentioned at that point in the text.

I   am   particularly indebted to my friend and
colleague John Whitehead for his help in shaping
chapter 2 and for his permission to quote freely
from his two books:

"Planning the Electronic Office", and "Implementing
the Electronic Office", both published by Croom
Helm.

I acknowledge, as always, the help give to me by my
wife in preparing and revising the manuscript.

P.J.Hills
Cambridge

1 THE ELECTRONIC REVOLUTION

In 1983 Kenneth Baker, then Minister for Educational Technology wrote:

> Information Technology is daily giving birth to new concepts, new products and new ideas, and radically transforming not only our industries and businesses but every aspect of our lives ...There is great potential for significant improvement in our lives as a result of the new technologies, but our ability to benefit from technological advance will depend entirely on the speed with which we adapt to it. (Baker, 1983)

The industrial revolution caused a tremendous change in the standards of living and affected many aspects of the lives of people in countries across the world. The industrial revolution brought people from the country to the town and cities, gathering them together in organisational structures of ever-increasing complexity in order to manufacture and market goods. Locations were initially based on the presence of raw materials, waterways, and/or the railways. People moved to where they were needed.

As Kenneth Baker has indicated we are now moving into what has been called variously a "second industrial revolution",or by some "a communications revolution" or an "electronic revolution". It is actually opposite in ethos to the industrial revolution in that it does not encourage the mass congregation of people, but rather, by a coming together of developments in telecommunications and computers, allows distributed working. Anyone can, theoretically, work from home, or indeed from any location, using telephone and microcomputer links to communicate with a central organisation, clients, suppliers or customers. When this possibility is added to the decline in the number

1

of jobs in manufacturing industries and the upsurge
of employment in the service industries, one begins
to see a substantial change in the way in which
people work.

The electronic revolution is both a social and an
economic revolution which in some way and in some
degree is affecting every aspect of our lives. Nor
must it be seen simply in terms of the creation of
work and jobs. Petrella, the Director of the
FAST(Forecasting and Assessment in Science and
Technology) Programme shows that hopes of new jobs
being created by the new technologies have been
"brutally put to the test by a number of studies"
(Petrella, 1984). He cites three main reasons for
this. First, he shows that hi-tech industries have
a relatively small base, second, that their
productivity will rise rapidly and the growth of
high-tech jobs will slow as those industries
automate production and, third, that there is a
tendency to use cheaper foreign labour for
non-skilled jobs. He foresees the emergence of a
new generation of "brainworkers" and believes that
the skills associated with the manual workers of
today will change considerably.

Petrella's analysis is useful in the context of
rationalising the individual as a working person.
He points out that although machines are capable of
replacing human resources, a working person is more
than, for example, a word processor and that the
other tasks he carries out in an organisation are
not only necessary but essentially "human".

> A working person is more than a
> "labour"factor ... He is a carrier of
> ethical and moral values; he has an
> "historical" patrimony and a culture behind
> and beyond his activity. A working person
> is primarily establishing linkages and
> interactions with other human persons
> within human organisations. (Petrella,1984)

He goes further in pointing out that the right to
life embraces the right and duty to work, the right
to paid work and the duty to do socially useful
work, even when not paid. He is demonstrating

2

essentially that work is only part of a world consisting of values and goals, a world in which the relationships between individuals, groups and organisations are what is important.

This is a theme which will be taken up and amplified in later chapters, since it is through such relationships that society transmits its values and standards in order to safeguard the existence of that society. The need to belong to groups and interact with others is an important aspect for us to consider in the educational process, but it must be placed in a wider context. In the past, "society" could be defined within the smaller boundaries of a community, a region or a country, where the numbers and types of groupings were comparatively, though not insignificantly, small. This picture of maintenance of values and standards is not now sufficient since today countries are joined by a network of virtually instant communication. Limitless sources of information are theoretically within our grasp. An incident happening in one part of the world can be on public television screens round the other side of the world within minutes. Heads of State and Heads of business can be kept up to date with developments as they happen, with the possibility of extrapolating probable trends very rapidly and in a way which was impossible only a few years ago.

As McHale puts it:

> In terms of information environment, our
> world has shrunk swiftly, in just over two
> generations, from one whose surface was
> still incompletely known and whose peoples
> were fairly remote strangers to one
> another, to one which is a continuous
> neighbourhood, in which, theoretically no
> person is more than a few hours distant
> from all others and in which communications
> may be practically instantaneous. (McHale,
> 1976)

Extensions of Man

Man's first extensions of himself were by the
drawing of pictures, in their simplest forms at
first which then became more complex. There
followed from this the development of writing, thus
enabling man to store information and retrieve it
from outside of himself. Twentieth century man has
vastly and with great speed extended this by using
a wide variety of techniques and devices to
communicate knowledge of culture and heritage, to
influence his fellow men and to store, process and
retrieve his communications.

Communication between human beings takes place via
the five senses of sight, hearing, taste, touch and
smell. The principal channels of communication are
sight and sound which embrace the printed word, the
visual image and the spoken word. Each of these has
developed both its own traditions and its own
methods for the presentation, storage and retrieval
of information. The electronic revolution,
representing as it does a coming together of
developments in microelectronics, optical fibres,
telecommunications, computers and satellites, is
revolutionising the treatment of words, pictures
and sound. By the use of one basic technology they
are being brought together in a digital form which
is capable of integrating them, storing them on a
common recording medium, and processing them in a
variety of ways - which would not have been
possible if non-electronic methods had been used -
and retrieving them with the capacity of being
sent quickly over vast distances with little or no
loss of quality.

This technology is leading to the establishment of
world-wide information networks where information
is theoretically available to all who desire it.
This is of course only theoretically possible,
because there are at present many barriers to this
total concept. These barriers range from matters of
cost and complexity to considerations of political
motivation and to tensions within and between
countries. There is however a much more vital and
basic consideration of which we have hardly begun

4

The Electronic Revolution

to conceive, much less tackle properly, namely the fact that children born in 1986 will be eighteen years of age in the year 2004 and will be reaping the rewards (whatever they may be) of what we do in the closing years of this century.

The basic question therefore is - What sort of educational system do we have now and what sort of educational system are we preparing for them?

The Present Educational System

The present educational system is under a considerable number of pressures. The following lists Government and non-government sources, industrial organisations etc. all of which exert influence on the present system.

Department of Education and Science
Department of Trade and Industry
Department of Employment
Department of Health and Social Security
Manpower Services Commission
Further Education Unit
The City and Guilds of London Institute
The Royal Society of Arts

The Technical and Vocational Educational Initiative
New Training Initiatives
The Business and Technican Education Council
Youth Training Schemes

School Curriculum Development Committee
Secondary Examinations Committee
Her Majesty's Inspectors

Local Examining Boards
Local Government
Non-Government Organisations
etc.

In the short term initiatives such as the Youth Training Scheme, the Technical and Vocational Educational Initiative, the new GCSE exam and a variety of pre- vocational courses are affecting educational organisations at all levels.

Although present educational initiatives are important and necessary at this stage of our thinking, it is necessary to look further ahead for, in the long term, as Williams puts it:

> Our lives and those of our children will be played out against a context of potentially overwhelming information, entertainment, and personal contact alternatives.

Williams suggests a number of implications of changes resulting from the electronic revolution. These are:

(1) a proliferation of the media channels.
   This will enable more personal choice of information and entertainment.

(2) time displacement.
   The increased use of video recorders and telephone answering machines illustrates the trend towards self-government of time rather than time schedules being imposed by others.

(3) increased mobility.
   Mobile phones and portable computers allow communication activities to be carried out using telephone and cellular radio networks.

(4) increased "connectivity".
   This is Williams´ way of expressing the ability to be "in touch" with a wide variety of communications alternatives. His concept can be extended to increased connectivity with others, by using a variety of spoken and written forms of communication.

He sees the survivors of these alternatives as those with "the wisdom to make the wisest choices among them."(Williams, 1984)

Each of these possible changes has implications for the way in which we implement the educational process and for the way in which we perceive the content and purpose of the process.

One important aspect of this is the need to develop in the individual an awareness of the problems of information overload, the ways in which information can and is being slanted to gain our attention and ways in which information can be handled. The other aspect of this is the increasing speed of technological change. As Toffler points out, because of this increase problems arise more rapidly than in the past and society is not capable of responding with the speed that is required. (Toffler, 1980) This means that an increasing proportion of society´s response to crises is made out of "desperation not deliberation". We have need of ways to plan for the future, anticipating problem areas and shaping events before they happen, a vital area which needs to be included in our consideration of the education of our future generations.

Education itself is an area where the pace of change is accelerating. Not only has the cost of education increased greatly in recent years, but, as we have begun to indicate above, the requirements for producing a suitable education for the future have also changed. Showing an individual the potential of learning how to learn may be the only certain way of anticipating the future. This re-emphasises the role of learner in education with the teacher as manager of the process.

The ways of conveying information to the learner have themselves become more complex as new methods constantly become available through technical developments in other areas. Computers are of course central to this, but a variety of developments such as interactive video, audio and teleconferencing are adding to this. The possibilities in presenting information are thus considerable but have not been matched by an understanding of the fundamentals of the learning process. However, future developments in artificial intelligence and expert systems may accelerate the rate of change in this area in the near future.

These words are being written during Industry Year 1986 and there is a tremendous concentration on the need to give students an awareness of the wealth creation process and of the part played by industry in maintaining our society. Many present educational initiatives are concerned with this and have as a central objective the need to create a skilled and flexible workforce. The danger in this is that it may be seen as the main objective of the educational process when in fact it is actually only one facet. Although important, it is subsumed and indeed extended if we place the focus of the educational process on the development of the individual in the context of self-growth, work, leisure and social awareness.

There is a great need at the present time for a "bottom up" approach to education rather than the more usual "top down" approach. That there is a growing need for this is evidenced by developments such as the Royal Society's "reduced science content" initiatives. Again, although still in a subject-based context this awareness ranges over more than just adjustment of subject content in the proposals for the GCSE. This is shown, for example, by statement of intent on aims and objectives in the National Criteria for this examination like the following in Biology and Business Studies:

Biology.

> To encourage an attitude of curiosity and scientific enquiry.

> To develop a range of manipulative and communication skills appropriate to the subject.

> To develop an ability to use these skills to identify and solve problems. (HMSO,1985)

Business Studies.

> To recognise, select, interpret and apply data.

> To organise information and apply it in an appropriate way to the solution of business

8

problems.

To promote knowledge and appreciation of
the working world and of the co-operation
and interdependence which participation in
society entails...

(HMSO,1985)

The need for education in communication skills and
life skills emerges clearly from these indications.
In following chapters aspects of these skills are
examined in relation to the needs and tasks of man
and his performance as an information processor.
Such skills are seen as basic pre-requisites to
considering how the introduction of the computer
can both enhance and extend these processes.

In all of this the teacher is seen as a necessary
mediator in the education process, but it must be
noted that at present the teaching profession is in
danger of turning in on itself. The present
attitude of teachers whereby they behave as though
the classroom were apart from the realities of a
changing world is compounded by a number of
factors, not the least of these being as follows:

Present school syllabuses are still
subject-based and concerned little with
processes for the maintainence of society
like wealth creation etc.

Teaching methods at present in use are not
sufficiently flexible to cope with the
range of ability in mixed classes.

Demands for education outside the formal
system are increasing, eg. the demands for
more relevant education, training and
retraining, life skills, communication
skills, continuing education needs etc.

Education can now take place outside of the
formal system, eg. the methods of

9

information technology, open learning,
distance learning, the Open University,
Open Tech. etc.

Many business and industrial organisations
are setting up their own education and
training units, using open learning and
information technology methods, eg.
Barclays Bank, Lloyds Bank, British
Petroleum, British Telecom.

Teachers at all levels must come to an increased
realisation that their task is not simply to relay
information to groups of students by lessons or
lectures. They should be concerned with the
self-development of the individual, shaping the
process in such a way that it will fit the
individual to play a productive part in helping to
control, direct and enhance our changing society.

In all of this we need to bear firmly in mind that

TEACHERS ARE NOT THE CUSTODIANS OF THE PAST, THEY
ARE GUARDIANS OF THE FUTURE.

If this book helps to focus teachers´ perceptions
of their task on this aim, then its purpose will
have been achieved.

2 COMPUTERS AND INFORMATION TECHNOLOGY

The industrial revolution laid stress on mindless mechanism, regarding work in terms of how much output a man could produce, and the maximum effort that one could get from him. The production line concept of work and effort has continued to shape the way we think about work and jobs. All previous developments shaped and dictated the ways in which we think about and use new developments, at least in their initial stages.

The use of computers can be shown to follow exactly this sort of development, since the first giant computers merely carried out complex mathematical calculations. Admittedly, they could be vastly more complex and faster than human calculators but they were still dealing with numbers, symbols and mathematical calculations. This type of usage could be traced directly from the abacus through Babbage's "mechanical computer" to our present pocket calculators, the computing power of which often equals or can exceed the early valve-based computers.

From this point there was a change of direction, and computers began to be used to process and manipulate text. It is the later development, allied with the coming together of developments in microcomputers, with increased sophistication of microprocessors and telecommunications generally that has led to the present electronic revolution. This in its turn is presenting us with the greatest and most exciting possibility for a quantum leap in the development of mankind, and of society in general, that we have ever known.

11

Information Technology.

It will be useful at this point to remind ourselves of the main points in the definition of Information Technology given in the introduction to this book:

> Information technology is the acquisition, production, transformation, storage and transmission of data by electronic means .... such as to facilitate the interaction between people, and between people and machines.
> (FEU, 1984)

We shall see later in this chapter how the computer and word processor can be linked to each other and to other devices to perform a whole variety of operations. The important point is that these operations can be performed anywhere, given the necessary equipment and a telephone line. They can be performed in the home, in the office, at school, in the library, virtually anywhere in the world. This leads to the concept of the "expanded organisation" in which, theoretically, all members can keep in touch with each other when transacting business, transmitting and receiving educational material and instruction etc., using the methods of Information Technology. However these methods affect the physical location of organisations, the organisations themselves will still need to carry out certain basic operations in order to transact their business. All organisations, whether they are business firms, educational establishments, or government agencies, are concerned with inputs and outputs, planning, decision making, staffing matters, administrative activities, - that is, communication both within and without the organisation.

Information Technology is beginning to be of assistance in these processes. However, before we begin to look in detail at computers and their component parts and interconnections, let us first look at scenarios representing actual or possible developments in everyday life, in the office and in education.

Information Technology and Everyday Life.

This can be illustrated by a real situation, the CLUB 403 experiment. This experiment was reported in Shirley's article "Social Consequences of the Electronic Revolution" (Shirley, 1984). The article described how a residential viewdata experiment involving domestic and educational users in Sutton Coldfield, Edgebaston and Solihull was set up. The service began with the intention of being information-based, but soon found that its service-based facilities like grocery shopping was a big success. The system offered access to news, sport, weather, local entertainment, leisure information, information on education and careers, travel and holidays, home shopping, a 24 hour banking system, social information etc.

Information Technology and the Office of the Future.

Sommerlatte (1982) envisages the office environment of the future as consisting of a linked system of communications including:

an electronic mail system,

a communications processor data network,

a data processing system,

an image communications system,

a PABX (Private Automatic Branch Exchange) voice network,

all interfaced with word processors, files, data terminals, copiers and telephones all linked to networks external to the firm. He sees the present office environment as typified by separate facilities but by 1990 in his prediction he foresees "the typical office environment will combine a multitude of capacities, either through the physical integration of the hardware at the

13

terminal and network levels or through the use of new multifunctional products and systems." (Sommerlatte, 1982)

Information Technology and the University of the Future.

The scenario for an "advanced" university of the 1990´s, as proposed by the Computer Board for Universities and Research Councils in a recent report, is as follows:

> All students have a portable personal computer of the power of an ICL Perq that can be connected to the local area network. All study bedrooms and library desks have connectors for the University Local Area Network. Fast, high quality printers are found in most university buildings. New tutorial and simulation software is produced by small teams including lecturers, computer centre programmer/analysts and educational technologists. These teams sometimes include academics at other universities who collaborate via inter-university network communications. The development cost of the new educational software is partly offset by sales of software licences. The part-time students make extensive use of the communications facilities to interact with other students and lecturers. Students studying vocational subjects (engineering, accountancy) use the communications network to use and carry out project work with contemporary applications, software. (CBURC,1983)

This type of scenario could well be extended to all aspects of work, leisure, education and society in general, in any situation where information is stored, transmitted, processed or received. What of the equipment that makes this possible and in particular what goes to make up a computer and how does it function?

Computers and Information Technology

The Computer

The rapid advances in the handling and processing
of information have arisen through developments in
microelectronics, computer technology and telecommunications. Developments in microelectronics
and the miniaturisation of electrical circuitry are
shown, for example, by the credit card sized pocket
calculator and the digital watch. The development
of integrated circuit technology is making it
possible for a silicon chip, itself only
millimetres across, to contain hundreds of
thousands of transistors.

Computers are basically a series of silicon chips
linked together, each with a different function.
The silicon chip which provides the central
processing unit for computers and other "computer"
controlled devices is known as the "microprocessor". Systems containing micro-processors are
being used to control the electrical systems in
cars, washing machines, cookers etc., etc. The
microprocessor is an integrated circuit which
contains the logic elements for manipulating data
and text, and for performing processing operations
on it. The microprocessor chip provides the
controls for the computer, decides what action to
take when a key is pressed, and controls the
display on the screen. The other chips include a
"ROM"(Read Only Memory) chip which provides
information to tell the computer what to do in
various circumstances. The "RAM"(Random Access
Memory) chip stores the information which the
microprocessor wants to keep.

This includes the computer program, the visual
display and information on the state of the
computer under particular conditions. The "ROM"
chip contains information which cannot be erased,
whereas information in the "RAM" chip can be erased
and new information stored. The chips are connected
by a logic chip which provides the input and output
circuitry to enable other devices needed by the
computer to be connected into the system. These
include the keyboard, the visual display screen,
disc drives (or other storage devices), a printer,
connection to the external telephone system etc.

Computers and Information Technology

What can computers do?

Computers allow you to:

    (1) Input data usually through a typewriter
        style keyboard.
    (2) See what you are doing on a
        television-like display screen.
    (3) Print out the results of your work or
        pieces of text on a printer of some
        kind.
    (4) Store your work on various types of
        magnetic storage media.
    (5) Communicate your work to other
        terminals or computers inside or
        outside your organisation.

Let us now examine each one of these in turn.

Input Devices.

Data is usually inputted to a computer using a conventional QWERTY typewriter-style keyboard. However, recently devices like the "mouse", the touch screen and the light pen have been introduced.

The "mouse"

This is a small box from the bottom of which protrudes a ball bearing. The bearing rotates as the user moves the mouse across a flat surface. This movement is transmitted down a cable which is linked to the computer and causes the cursor to move across the screen. When the cursor moves to a function displayed on the screen such as "store", "print", "graphics" etc. a button on the mouse is pressed and the function is activated.

The touch screen

This is a Hewlett Packard innovation introduced in 1984 on their 100 series microcomputer. It enables you to touch any part of the display screen to

16

you to touch any part of the display screen to
activate a given function. A matrix of invisible
microwave beams emanating from holes along the
edges criss-cross the display screen. By pressing
your finger against a function displayed on the
screen the beam is broken at that intersection and
the system is activated.

The light pen

This uses a laser beam to "read" information stored
on a bar chart. A similar device can be used to
read off information from a thin strip of magnetic
material. This type of system is used to keep stock
records, check costs etc.

Two other main types of input device, the optical
character reader and voice input are in the process
of development.

Optical Character Recognition (OCR)

These systems are capable of reading text and then
storing that text in a computer storage system.
Typereaders use a photoelectric cell to scan each
line of text, identifying and transcribing each
character of the text, and, once recognised, the
character can be displayed or transferred to the
computer's storage system. Banks use a typeface
known as "OCR A" to print the cheque number,
account number and bank sort number on the bottom
of cheques so that they can be read directly on to
the computer.

The advantages of OCR systems will be very obvious
since an increasing problem for all who work with
information is how to store and retrieve the large
amount of printed material which comes from
outside. To be able to transfer it on to the
in-house system would have many advantages but
unfortunately there are so many different types of
typeface in existence that a typereader to cope
with all possibilities has yet to be developed.

Voice Input

A voice-operated typewriter appears in Asimov's

Science Fiction Foundation trilogy but the little girl operating it, Arkady Darrell, soon discovers the difference between the spoken word and the varieties of spelling of the written word.

The machine is described as follows:

> It will spell and punctuate correctly according to the sense of the sentence. Naturally it is a great aid to education since it encourages the user to employ careful enunciation and breathing in order to make sure of the correct spelling, to say nothing of demanding a proper and elegant delivery for correct punctuation.

Arkady's first essay using the machine contained the following sentence:

> Through the science of psychohistory the intrissacies of whose mathematics have been forgotten..., (She paused in a trifle of doubt. She was sure that 'intricacies' was pronounced with soft c's but the spelling didn't look right. Oh, well, the machine couldn't very well be wrong ..." (Asimov, 1953).

In reality even the development of such a system is difficult since speech has to be programmed in such a way that the computer can recognise what it hears, and different languages and regional dialects are difficult to cope with. Voice activated systems are being developed but so far can cope only with clearly enunciated speech using a relatively limited vocabulary.

Output Devices

Display Screens

These vary from the sort of liquid crystal displays used in portable computers and pocket calculators to the high definition colour monitors used with high quality computer systems. Although the quality of a picture displaying text and graphics is very much better on a Visual Display Unit (VDU) than it is if a computer were to be connected to a domestic television set, it still suffers from the problems of flicker inherent in the system of line scanning used in a cathode ray tube. Operator problems like eye strain and posture problems can result from working too long at such screens.

Very high definition screens are being developed and experiments with different colour combinations for text and background colour have been carried out. At the present time a green background colour with yellow text is thought to be a restful yet clear combination. Work is also going on to produce flat display screens, the nearest approach to this at present being the liquid crystal displays previously mentioned.

The main limitation of a display screen at present is that for all practical purposes it is a linear device showing one screenful of information followed by another in a linear progression. On the other hand, paper-based systems are much more flexible; as I write I have on the surface of my desk, the equivalent of eight full A4 pages of text visible for scanning. Attempts have been made to overcome the linear presentation of text by computer. The ability to "scroll" text across a screen like the closing titles of a television programme is one method in use at the moment. Attempts have been made to use a split screen or reserve portions of a screen for specific pieces of information but for the most part these are limited by the size of screen available. To achieve the effect of the papers at present available on my desk, one would need a screen at least six feet by four feet, or an order of magnitude larger if the screen were any greater distance from me. The problem of high definition obviously becomes more acute as the size of screen increases.

Printers.

Printers can broadly be divided into impact printers and non-impact printers.
Impact printers range from cheap dot matrix printers to those of letter quality using a "daisy

wheel" to give the equivalent of high quality typewriter lettering. Some form of striking device transfers ink from an inked ribbon on to the paper to form the characters. Dot matrix printers, introduced in the early 1970´s use wire pins which strike the ribbon against the paper in the pattern necessary to build up each character. Although not of high letter print quality, they can be used to print a large range of typefaces and can also print graphics, drawings etc. With suitable inking they can be used to print colour. One finds these dot matrix printers connected with many microcomputers.

Letter print quality printers use daisy wheels, golfballs etc. which contain characters ready formed. They strike the ribbon like a hammer and transfer the image to the paper. Daisy wheels, for example, consist of a number of stalks radiating from a central core. Each stalk has one character at the end of it. These printers work by rotating the wheel so that the correct character is uppermost, a small hammer then strikes the back of the stalk so that the character strikes the ribbon, printing it on to the paper.

Non-impact printers include thermal printers which use heated dot matrix pins pressing against a special heat sensitive paper, and ink jet printers which spray a jet or jets of ink on to the paper in patterns to form the characters. Laser printers have recently been introduced which combine the use of a laser with the xerographic principle. Here a laser beam scans across a charged xerographic selenium drum to build up an electrostatic image of the text. Toner is then attracted to the electrostatic image; it is transferred to paper and fixed permanently by heat, employing the usual xerographic technique.

Storage Devices.

Data storage devices for computers can range from simple audio-tape recorders, to computer tape or floppy disks, ranging in sizes from 3.5" to 8" in diameter. Hard Winchester disks with a very large storage capacity are now becoming popular.

Computers and Information Technology

Audiotape cassette recorders are perhaps the cheapest way of storing information from a computer and are used with many home computers. However, information so stored takes a long time to load into the computer and is in addition not as easy to retrieve as with disk systems.

Floppy disks are perhaps the most popular, relatively cheap system in use. The disks are made of a soft plastic material coated with a compound on which the information is stored magnetically. These disks exist in various forms and sizes, so allowing the storage of varying amounts of information.

Winchester hard disks are in units, sealed to exclude all dust which could otherwise affect the storage of information, and cannot be removed from the computer. These metal disks spin very rapidly and once filled to capacity they are either used for long term storage of the information or are erased to be used again. There are various other hard disk storage systems and recently an optical disc has been developed. Such disks hold tremendous advantages for the storage of data. Capacities to hold images of 50,000 or more pages of text, pictures, diagrams etc. have been quoted. This information can be read by using an optical laser system.

Processing text and communication functions.

In addition to performing mathematical calculations and storing or retrieving information, computers can perform a variety of operations. Two of their major functions are processing text and sending and receiving messages. These are dealt with below.

Processing Text

Text can be processed, that is, typed in, edited, corrected, transposed etc., by using a computer which has a word processing function. Many organisations, at present, use systems known as

21

"word processors". These are basically micro-computers which are dedicated to, that is, devoted entirely to, the specific task of word processing. The phrase "word processing" comes from the name "Textverarbeitung" used by the German subsidiary of IBM in the 1960´s to describe their new range of correcting typewriters. This phrase is now used to describe text processing systems in general. A word processor can be described as a computerised electronic typewriter with some additional functions. It still uses a QWERTY keyboard and has all the usual functions of a typewriter but in addition usually has a wide range of type founts with the possibility of proportional spacing, a display screen, a means of storing information on floppy disks etc., a communications facility that enables one to use them as computer terminals.

Most word processors now include facilities to provide:

> the storage and retrieval of information
> search and sort facilities
>
> electronic mail/ message switching systems
>
> access to in-house and external computers
>
> access to telex/teletex and other
> communication links (see below).

Manufacturers extended the facilities of their machines to include a wide range of options which are usually associated with computers. Computer manufacturers realised that word processors were penetrating their markets and began to provide word processing facilities for their computers. Hence we have a convergence of what were initially two rather different devices which can now perform basically the same types of operation.

Sending and Receiving Messages.

Computer-linked Communication Facilities.

Increasing use is being made of such systems, even

though one of the major problems has been the incompatability of different makes of equipment. Although some conversion devices have been produced to overcome this between certain makes of microcomputers, word processors and office computer systems, this is still a major problem. Between compatable types of equipment, however, there are various ways of achieving communication. Perhaps the most significant development has been the networking of systems. This enables microcomputers to link together to share facilities such as printers, telex, teletex, large capacity storage units and general communications facilities. This is achieved by linking the computers into a local area network (LAN). In simple terms LAN's can be equated to the electricity ring mains in a house. It is a cable system enabling various devices to share central facilities. LAN's offer a simple yet flexible approach. These networks could be no more than a loop of wire around an organisation. Plug-in sockets are located at convenient places so that the devices can be plugged in. Thus each workstation is provided with immediate access to central or shared facilities on the system, allowing, in this way, each work station to communicate with the other.

Computers can also be linked to telex and teletex facilities by using public telephone networks. They can also link into electronic mail and message switching systems, they can access information from a variety of databases, and they can "talk" to other compatable computers across the world.

Telecommunications Systems

Telecommunications, the means of communicating over long distances, has itself undergone tremendous developments, not the least of these being the introduction of communication satellites. By means of telephone cables, optical fibre cables, radio and television links and communication satellites, communication by sound, picture or computer is possible virtually anywhere in the world. Prestel, viewdata systems and a vast variety of computer databases are available and can be linked to office based or home based systems.

The major means of communication is still through the telephone network. Improvements in telephones using handsets with automatic dialling and redialling are well known and a variety of other features are available, including telephone answering devices, telephones which can be carried about without cables and cellular radio telephones. Conference phone facilities are perhaps one of the most interesting developments from the educational point of view. Here three or more people are linked by telephone so that they can speak to each other. For anyone wishing to follow this up in more detail, a recent article (Winders, 1985) describes the PACNET system at Plymouth Polytechnic.

Text Systems

There are a number of these available, some of which are well established such as telex and facsimile transmission systems. More recent systems include electronic mail and teletex.

Electronic Mail

This is actually a general term used to describe a whole range of electronic communication systems including telex, teletex facsimile transmission, and computer-based communication facilities such as electronic message systems, voice mail etc. A number of bureaux offer electronic mail services of which the most extensive UK service is "BT Gold" operated by British Telecom. "Prestel", the British Telecom videotext service which gives access to a variety of information pages, also offers an electronic mail facility. For this system a computer is unnecessary. All that is needed is a Viewdata terminal, a telephone access interface, a Prestel membership number and a password.

Telex

Telex was introduced over 50 years ago and links many companies and organisations around the world. As the cost of using telex is based on the time spent sending the message, costs can be quite high if the message is keyed-in manually during transmission. The use of punched paper tape or magnetic storage to pre-record messages has speeded up transmission time. Modern switching systems link electronic office equipment into a shared telex network which cuts down user time and delay in access. Facilities include storage of incoming and outgoing messages in computer storage devices, allowing automatic dialling, with messages being transmitted in sequence or being held in memory until required.

Teletex

Teletex is similar to telex but operates at a much higher speed and with a more conventional character set than telex. It also works through the normal telephone network rather than through the special telex system. Whereas telex messages use capital letters and telegram-like abbreviations, teletex can transmit text prepared on microcomputers etc. in the normal way. At the moment Telex and Teletex are both being maintained. Teletex has been described as the text transmission system of the 1990´s and will eventually replace telex systems.

Facsimile Transmission(Fax)

Fax is a method of transmitting a facsimile copy of a document or drawing from one location to another by means of the telephone network. Fax machines operate by scanning the document in a series of narrow lines which are converted into signals of varying amplitude or frequency and are transmitted down the telephone line to be received and reconverted into a facsimile copy of the document at the other end. In order to do this, when first connected, the two machines "talk" to each other to ensure that they are compatable and that they are set at the same speed and mode.

Copy quality varies with the type of machine. With the new equipment available copies of text, diagrams, drawings etc. can be transmitted at reasonable cost. Although text is converted into electrical impulses by this method it does not do it by individual character recognition and so is of

no use for the OCR computer devices described earlier. Thus text captured in this way cannot be submitted to text editing processes etc, it can only be reproduced as scanned.

Viewdata

Viewdata is a name given to an interactive system which enables users to access a computer through the normal telephone service, displaying computer information on their own television screen. Using Viewdata users can access a wide range of information supplied by many companies and organisations (called "providers") who buy time on the system to display their services.

In the UK the public viewdata service is called Prestel and is operated by British Telecom. Most of the facilities provided carry no charge from British Telecom but some providers levy a charge on users who access their data, and this is billed by British Telecom on a quarterly basis. Prestel also has a closed user facility which enables various organisations to use the system as an in-house information service or electronic mail service. Security passwords are used to allow these users access to the parts of the system which are reserved for them.

Databases

Using a microcomputer or a communicating terminal and a telephone line, it is now possible to access a wide variety of databases to obtain information on most subjects, articles, books, conference papers etc. This is often the way in which libraries now obtain their information if it is not available in their own system.

Some of the better-known database services are those of "Datastream", which provides financial information, "Predicasts", which provides a wide range of statistics and lists various forecasts and estimates for markets, products and services from a wide range of sources, and "Lexis" which provides a wide range of legal information.

Other communication links include travel agent booking services for airlines and hotel reservation systems. Commercial organisations such as banks also use this type of communication link for electronic fund transfer between their members on a strictly private basis.

These then are the computers, word processors and devices that form the core around which Information Technology is built and which are influencing our lives in so many ways. Before we begin to explore some of these in relation to their educational implications, the next chapter looks at the aims of education and its present projects and initiatives in order to set the educational scene.

3 THE PRESENT EDUCATIONAL SCENE

The eighteen-year-olds of the year 2000 are with us
today and next year (1987) will begin their period
of formal education. Now is the time to put these
questions, are we still educating for a "sabre-
toothed curriculum" (see Hills, 1985, page 2), or
are we addressing the fundamental question of what
the world will be like in the years following the
year 2000? Educators and those responsible for
education should already be concerning themselves
with this question and should be beginning to
build into the system an awareness of the
possibilities. This change is coming upon us at a
time when there is a drop in the number of pupils
entering school, drastic cuts in educational
expenditure, teachers' unrest and, seemingly, a
general turning-in of schools upon themselves. This
is a time when we should be looking outwards to
meet the challenges and to provide education which
is both relevant and timely for our changing
society.

This general turning-in upon themselves may be a
manifestation of the level at which teachers are
operating in Maslow's hierarchical needs structure
(see chapter 4), since in a period of retrenchment
and anxiety about salary levels there is bound to
be a tendency to regress to basic security need
levels and not to look outwards at the wider needs
of the educational system for the benefit of
society. Michael Duffy, Headmaster of a 13 to 18
Comprehensive Community School, has said of the
present situation:

> ...there's a paradox. We are educating for
> the future, but we are not very good at
> looking into the future ourselves. We have
> assumed, not unreasonably, that the future
> will look after itself. In any case, as any
> teacher will tell you, we need a period of

> stability and retrenchment. We´re punch
> drunk with change. Comprehensive
> reorganisation, the raising of the school
> leaving age, equal opportunity, the
> mousetrap-like saga of the reform of
> examinations at 16+, falling rolls,
> profiles, pre-vocational education, the
> Youth Training Scheme ... all have made
> heavy demands on our resilience and our
> energy. (Duffy,1984)

There will, however, be no period of stability
during which we can examine our problems in a
leisurely way. We need to think on our feet at a
time when change is pressing upon us on all sides .
At the present time, and perhaps because of the
pressure of short term needs, it seems that no
attempts are being made to look at the problem in
an integrated way and to try to implement
solutions based on this. The old management adage
concerning crisis management makes the point that
you cannot think of draining the swamp when you are
up to your neck in alligators.

This book sets out not to drain the swamp but to
draw attention at least to where the plug is and
perhaps to loosen it a little. To do this we need
to look at the present views of what education is
for, examine present pressures on the system and
then see how things are changing in the light of
the electronic revolution, and finally to come to
some tentative conclusions for further action.

The Aims of Education

Although given in the context of higher education
the Robbins Report (HMSO 1963) gave four basic
statements which could be considered as the aims of
education at any level and which were "essential to
any properly balanced system". These statements
were:

> (1) to provide instruction in skills
>   suitable to play a part in the general
>   division of labour

(2) to teach in such a way as to promote the general powers of the mind

(3) to further the advancement of learning

(4) to transmit a common culture and common standards of citizenship.
(Robbins,1963)

Since these aims have been reaffirmed in the recent Green Paper "The Development of Higher Education in the 1990´s" (DES,1985), we can perhaps be justified in considering them to be the best expression of the purpose of education at the present time. Together with a concern for instruction in such skills in order to fit people for employment, and a concern for the furtherance of society and the development of the individual, there was one important additional emphasis. The Green Paper was concerned particularly with making sure that education gave a greater awareness of the process of wealth creation and greater links with and appreciation of the role of industry and commerce.

Awareness of Industry

Making the formal education system more aware of industry and its importance to society is a theme reflected in statements from a number of leading industrialists, for example, Sir Dennis Rooke, Chairman of British Gas, speaking to the Standing Conference on Schools´ Science and Technology, took as his theme "Education: Investment in Human Assets", and focused on the future citizen as technician, innovator and consumer:

I suspect that few would disagree with the White Paper "Training for Jobs" when it says that "Britain lives by the skill of its people" and "A well-trained workforce is an essential condition of our economic survival..."

30

What are the causes of this massive decline
in the UK´s manufacturing capability? No
one factor can be singled out. If it could,
it would be much easier to find a solution.

Lack of competitiveness is not itself a
single factor, but it is an amalgam of high
prices, long and uncertain delivery dates,
faulty products and poor marketing at the
output end of the business; and by lack of
innovation, inadequate attention to design,
rather rigid manning practices, poorly
trained manpower, expensive materials and
inefficient machinery at the input end. It
is a truly interdisciplinary problem
demonstrating a lack of the right adaptable
skills at all levels of industry.... we
cannot afford expensive learning curves in
industrial production; we must get it
nearly right at the outset. Education is
now essential to both innovation and to
implementation. (Rooke, 1984)

Sir Kenneth Durham, Chairman of Lever Brothers,
speaking at an International Conference of Higher
Education at the University of York in 1984 was
concerned both with wealth creation and the
innovation process in industry. His comments
reflect on restrictions placed by society and the
formal education system on individuals and
organisations. He proposed that although we are not
"an unenterprising nation" the reason for our lack
of economic success may be due to factors which
include:

"our dilatory response to technical
change..an aversion to risk taking...an
educational system inimical to industry."

He emphasised that:

"the understanding by academics and
educationalists of wealth creation seems
inadequate."(Durham, 1984)

The Present Educational Scene

Response to These Concerns

The Royal Society of Arts (RSA)

This society, founded in 1754 for the purpose of
the encouragement of arts, manufactures and
commerce, has been particularly active in
recognising the effect that information technology
is having on all aspects of work and leisure and
has engaged in a number of activities in connection
with this. One particular RSA initiative was to
launch 1986 as Industry Year. Three areas of action
have been identified with the objective of
encouraging a better understanding of industry, its
essential role and its service to the community.
These are:

(1) Increasing public awareness of industry's
    role

(2) Accelerating change in the relationship
    between education and industry

(3) Encouraging industry to explain the part
    that it plays in society.

The Society is attempting to link schools with
local industry and to develop industry links with
higher and further education. These links include
the arrangement of various "Industry Weeks" and a
network of local and regional activities, and it
also has the aim of involving industry more in the
initial and in-service training of teachers to
stimulate an awareness of the role and the
importance of industry in society.

Sir Geoffrey Chandler, Chairman of the Industry
Year Campaign writing in the magazine "Linkup",
lays the source of industry's problems firmly at
education's door when he says:

> ...what we define as the causes of our
> relative industrial failure are in fact
> symptoms of a deeper cause. They are
> symptoms of an inherited culture and a set
> of attitudes which put industrial activity
> at the bottom of the social pecking order

> and of an educational system which by
> ignoring or denigrating it, obscures the
> connection between the quality of life and
> industrial success. (Chandler, 1986)

He supports this view by referring to a survey
commissioned by the Committee for Research into
Public Attitudes which found that only one-third of
secondary school pupils would choose to work in
industry or commerce, and he points to this work of
the RSA´s "Education for Capability" and the
Society of Education Officers´ "School Curriculum
Award" as indicative of the fact that the
educational system "is more open to change than it
has ever been". The message is therefore very clear
both from government, from industry and from
support given by commissions like the RSA. What of
the implementation? What is actually happening in
schools, colleges, polytechnics and universities?
Michael Duffy says "we´re punch drunk with change".
The reality would seem to support this.

There are many initiatives, all of which would seem
to carry the same basic message:

> (1) Education must be more aware of change,
> and must itself change to take account of
> the changing needs of society.

> (2) Education must take more account of
> industry and its value to society, and
> should become more work related.

Details of some of these initiatives are given
below to illustrate the complexity and overlay.

Manpower Services Commission.(MSC)

To this effect a variety of Government initiatives
have been mounted, one of the principal
developments being that by the Manpower Services
Commission through projects such as the Youth
Training Scheme and Open Tech.

The Present Educational Scene

The Open Tech. Programme was launched in 1982 for the purpose of extending the training opportunities available to adults by identifying needs for training, and retraining and updating in skills and knowledge. Its stated aims are to focus on people in or seeking to return to employment with technician and supervisory level skills, filling specific present and future skill shortages. It is also intended particularly to help people to face up to the consequences of change in their work.

The Youth Training Scheme, now extended to two years, was originally introduced as a one-year scheme in 1983 to combine education and work experience, with students spending part of their time in industry and part in school.

The Technical and Vocational Initiative (TVEI) which is designed to provide educational courses for students between the ages of 14 and 18 has also been initiated by the MSC. It thus offers an opportunity for both general education and the chance of work experience.

The Business and Technician Education Council

In a similar way the Business and Technician Education Council (BTEC) also works to advance the quality and availability of a wide range of employment-related education, promoting the provision of education "which meets the changing needs of industry, commerce and the public services and which provides students with an intellectual challenge." BTEC have joined with the City and Guilds of London Institute (CGLI) to form The Joint Board for Pre-Vocational Education "to establish joint arrangements for a system of pre-vocational education on a national basis, including 17+ qualifications."

This has led to the establishment of a Certificate of Pre-Vocational Education (CPVE) which is a one-year full-time course for students who have not yet decided on a job and which involves a balance of core studies and vocational studies, learning through practical experience, planned work experience and guidance and support on careers.

The Joint Board themselves recognise the problem of overlap and, in their consultative document, have expressed their concern about relationships between CPVE and TVEI in the following words:

> An increasing number of pupils in recent years have been undertaking, in their final year of comprehensive schooling, courses such as CGLI Foundation and Vocational Preparation(General). With the introduction of TVEI, interest in these and similar schemes is increasing both pre and post 16 as LEA´s design their 14-18 progressions.
>
> Whilst CPVE will subsume these schemes post-16 they will be continued to be offered pre-16. The problem of repetition and of obscurity of route between the CPVE and pre-16 courses will be created.
> (BTEC,1984)

Further Education Curriculum Review and Development Unit

The Further Education Curriculum Review and Development Unit(FEU) is an example of a Government body set up in 1977 to act as an advisory intelligence and development body specifically in the area of further education. It has been very active in the field and is particularly concerned with educational relevance:

> For many young people, if education is to mean something to them and to be seen of value by them, the educational process must be useful and instrumental in developing skills for work and adult life. A skills-based curriculum with a relevant vocational focus often provides the right kind of stimuli for the young person to experience the wider aims of education.(FEU,1982)

This statement is expanded into a checklist of

35

twelve aims. This list is of particular interest in the context of this chapter since it shows not only a concern for the development of what might be called "work skills" but also concern for the development of the whole person so that he or she may be fitted to take a place in contemporary society. Education should thus bring about:

(1) an informed perspective as to the role and status of a young person in an adult society and the world of work

(2) a basis from which the young person can make an informed and realistic decision with respect to his or her immediate future

(3) a continuing development of physical and manipulative skills, in both vocational and leisure contexts, and an appreciation of those skills in others

(4) an ability to develop satisfactory personal relationships with others

(5) a basis on which the young person acquires a set of moral values applicable to issues in contemporary society

(6) a level of achievement in literacy and numeracy appropriate to ability and adequate to meet the basic demands of contemporary society

(7) competence in a variety of study skills which are likely to be demanded of the young person

(8) a capacity to approach various kinds of problems methodically and effectively,

and to plan and evaluate courses of
action

(9) sufficient political and economic
literacy to understand the social
environment and participate in it

(10) an appreciation of the physical and
technological environments, and the
relationship between these and the
needs of man in general and working
life in particular

11) a development of the everyday coping
skills necessary to promote
self-sufficiency in the young people

12) a flexibility of attitude and
willingness to learn sufficiently to
cope with future changes in technology
and career.(FEU,1982)

These aims although written in the context of
further education can bear at all levels close
examination, in relation to the needs of society
and our present educational system.

FEU also play a major part in the Department of
Education and Science's PICKUP programme which is
part of the Government's adult training
initiatives. PICKUP (Professional, Industrial and
Commercial Updating) is designed to encourage
further and higher educational establishments to
enter what has been for them an unfamiliar field -
adult updating. There are four key elements in the
programme:

(1) the establishment of a data base of
PICKUP provisions across the country

(2) a network of Regional Development
Agents to support and encourage PICKUP
developments

(3) a programme of PICKUP curriculum
development projects

(4) seminars, workshops and training sessions
for staff and officials involved in PICKUP

The Regional Development Agents assist staff in
colleges both to develop PICKUP-type provisions and
to make the best use of existing course materials
and funding sources. FEU has commissioned a number
of PICKUP development projects and has in
particular highlighted marketing adult updating as
an area in which to run a series of regional
workshops. The Newcastle Micro Systems Centre is an
example of a PICKUP project which has developed
microcomputer software in the area of database
provision in order to allow colleges to compile
data bases of local employers´ needs for PICKUP.

The Schools Council

The Schools Council was perhaps the body most
concerned with schools, curriculum change and
planning. It was formally closed down in March 1984
and replaced by two organisations, the School
Curriculum Development Committee (SCDC),
established in December 1983, and the Secondary
Examination Council (SEC). Although it may seem
that I am using this as a further illustration of
the complexity, overlap and needless duplication of
initiatives, this development seems to have been a
sensible rationalisation of two strands of Schools
Council work, namely examination business (taken
over by SEC, see under "GCSE" below) and the
review, evaluation and promotion of curriculum
development work (taken over by SCDC). This latter
body has given support to certain of the Schools
Council projects and the dissemination of completed
ones.

In an initial statement the SCDC showed its
awareness of the problems now facing many schools:

...the Committee has been very conscious of
current realities, and recognises that
schools, teachers and pupils are working in

38

a context of economic constraint,
unemployment, falling roles, new
technologies and changing provision for
educational and vocational training. These
and other social changes create both
opportunities and problems for education;
through its unique national perspective,
the committee wishes to offer practical
support and encouragement to the work of
LEA´s and teachers.(SCDC,1984)

Its concerns have however been largely
conventionally school based , a fact that is made
evident by the following themes which it identified
for early consideration:

Personal and social education, including
the preparation of pupils for adult life.

Mathematics- implementation of the
recommendations of the Cockcroft report.

Communication Skills... in relation to
pupils´ conceptual development and their
need to express increasingly complex ideas
to a variety of audiences.

Aesthetic Education - seeking an improved
education in drama, music, visual arts,
literature and dance in schools...

Assessment and Examinations - working
closely with the Secondary Examinations
Council on the curricular implications of
current work on assessment and
examinations, in the context of the
developing criteria for 16+. (SCDC,1984)

Examining Board Initiatives

The school examining boards have been looking at a
range of methods and possibilities, including
profiles and norm-referenced testing, and in some
cases they have proposed alternative certification.

The Present Educational Scene

The Oxford Certificate of Educational Achievement is one example of this. It consists of three components, a "P", a "G" and an "E" component.

The P-component takes the form of a personal record which draws on the formative experiences articulated by the student and teachers in all curriculum areas, and is compiled by the student in consultation with the teacher.

The G-component is a detailed statement of what the student has achieved. Progress is recognised as it occurs and the student is able to identify learning objectives and establish his progress within the curriculum.

The E-component records all external examination results eg. GCSE, BTEC, CGLI etc, achieved throughout the student's career.

The General Certificate of Secondary Education

Perhaps the major initiative at school level is the introduction of a new single system of examinations at 16+ known as the General Certificate of Secondary Education (GCSE) which replaces the GCE "O" Level, CSE, and joint 16+ exams in England and Wales from Summer 1988.

> The Secondary Examinations Council is responsible for ensuring that all GCSE examination syllabuses, in all modes, and all assessment, moderation, grading and certification procedures comply with the national criteria and that standards are comparable across different subjects and Examining Groups and over time... All GCSE syllabuses, assessment procedures and examinations will comply with the "National Criteria" as approved by the Secretaries of State for Education and Science and the Welsh Office in January 1985. (HMSO,1985)

Existing GCE and CSE Boards have been grouped together into five groups for the purpose of administrating the new examination. The groups are:

London and East Anglia
Southern
Northern
Midland
Wales

Grades are awarded on a seven point scale A to G, with GCE Boards having a special repsonsibility within the Groups for maintaining standards A to C and CSE Boards being concerned with grades D to G.

The Government´s stated intention in this examination is "to improve the quality of education and raise the standards of attainment by stretching and stimulating pupils throughout the ability range."(HMSO,1985)

It was also felt that the examination would produce a system which set clear targets and motivated pupils and staff.

Changing the Educational System.

All this present activity can be seen as being composed of a variety of initiatives taken in response to the recognition that there is a problem with our present educational system and that it should and must change. In the account above,one of the principal arguments for change has been the need to educate for a greater appreciation of industry and the process of wealth creation. It is interesting, therefore, to note a prediction by Stonier writing in 1983:

Within 30 years it will take no more than 10% of the labour force to produce all of society´s needs. That is, all the food, clothing, textiles, furniture, appliances, automobiles, housing etc....(Stonier,1983)

Even if Stonier is wrong in his percentage, the truth of his prediction is already apparent in the trends of employment figures for manufacturing industries as compared with service industries.

41

The Present Educational Scene

This might be interpreted as merely a switch from
one type of job to another. However, while it is
true that there has been an upsurge of jobs in the
service industries, it is also true that
increasingly the service industries will require a
smaller labour force as the use of computers etc.
removes the more routine tasks. Similarly robots,
computers and other automated devices will continue
to reduce the number of tasks available to an
unskilled work force in the manufacturing
industries. It seems therefore likely that this
trend will continue even if there were to be a
massive recovery in the world economic situation.

The changes taking place in employment are those
away from the unskilled or semi-skilled,
repetitive, hazardous types of job towards jobs
which require more thought. Thus there will
continue to be a trend towards higher unemployment,
or, looked at another way, there will the
possibility of fewer hours employment per person
per year.

With the increased use of computers and automation
there is also an increased opportunity for people
to be employed or to work in areas of human and
community concern.

Petrella makes a distinction between employment and
work when he defines employment from the point of
view of the employers where human beings are
considered as resources "to be used in the context
of the optimisation of the production function".
Work is defined as "an activity carried out by a
person, whether paid or not, to satisfy his own and
society's needs by the production, distribution and
consumption of goods and services." As I mentioned
in an earlier chapter, he carries the idea further
when he goes on to say, "the right to life embraces
and justifies the right and duty to work, the right
to do paid work and the duty to do socially useful
work (even if not paid)." (Petrella,1984)

Human beings are essentially gregarious creatures.
Only by mixing with and talking to others can they
completely maintain mental health and a balanced

42

personal perspective of the world they live in. Since the opportunity now exists to use computers and robots, thus freeing people from the routine task of life and work, this can result in giving the whole population more time to think, to develop higher skills and to involve themselves in community programmes.

The decreasing opportunities for employment, the need for higher skills and the increase in time to do other things all pose considerable problems for the individual who for the most part is still steeped in the tradition of the Protestant work ethic.

At the present time it is the under-25´s who make up about a quarter of all the long-term unemployed. Those in this age range have little to sustain them, since they have had no opportunity to aquire previous working habits, self-discipline, or ways of filling their total leisure time. This lack of anything to do may lead to destructive acts or attitudes towards society. As Dutton et al. comment:

> If an individual perceives "worth" only when (s)he is commissioned to do something on behalf of others, unemployment will lead to the destruction of the self-image unless the person concerned can use the (enforced) leisure time creatively and successfully. (Dutton et al. 1984)

This then is one of our challenges, that we should switch the individual´s concept of education as being something simply to fit him for employment. Rather he needs to regard this concept as a preparation for and involvement in life. This is not a new concept. Educators have long held this as an ideal. Now it must become a reality. It must become a reality in a world where people interact much more with computers, where work is no longer necessarily in one place and can be based in the home with computer links to a central organisation. All of this is likely to contribute to less person-to-person contact. Consequent factors of social isolation must also be considered in our educational equation since personal contact with others is an essential pre-requisite of the human condition.

This is not to undervalue the variety of present initiatives and their impact on the educational situation. Indeed it may be that such a variety of initiatives has been necessary to shake educationalists and others out of their well established routines and that this has been one way of doing it.

Whether one sees this programme of largely unco-ordinated change agents descending on the present educational system as a necessary thing, or whether one deplores the waste of effort when a focused thrust might have led us all to the same point much quicker, matters little at this present time. All of the initiatives described above and more exist and are working their way into and through our educational system. We cannot stop the process, but we can examine what has happened so far in relation to our future concerns and attempt to formulate a coherent and flexible educational continuum.

4 THE NEEDS AND TASKS OF MAN

In order that we may be able to educate for, and
take account of, a changing world we ought to look
more closely at the basic needs of man himself,
(the internal needs), and at the tasks of man
imposed on him by society, (the external needs). In
this way we can perhaps begin to discover what our
own tasks as educators should consist of. With
these in mind, let us first consider the external
needs.

The External Needs.

The population of the world is formed into
interacting groups, societies of people who to a
greater or lesser extent exist as integrated
self-organising systems. These groups are made up
of individuals who can themselves be thought of as
self-organising systems. Thus, as individuals, they
have needs which should be fulfilled in order that
they may maintain themselves; and they, in their
turn, must undertake a variety of tasks in order to
maintain the needs of the society in which they
live and work. These tasks enable man to maintain
himself, his family and the immediate circle of
people connected with him. In our present society
man must work to earn money by playing his part in
some organisation, business or industry which, in
turn, plays a part in the wealth creation process
of society. There are however further tasks which
man should undertake for the benefit of the
community and himself. Voluntary service to help to
maintain the caring and community aspects of
society, either locally or on a larger scale, is
one important aspect of this, but there is another
equally important aspect. It is this. In order to
work man must also play, since play relaxes
tensions and gives opportuntiy for creative and
renewing activities.

These three aspects should be borne in mind when considering man and his actions in society, but here we shall concentrate only on the tasks carried out in connection with the playing of his part in the wealth creation process of society.

Organisations, whether they are business, industrial, or educational, all have common characteristics. First, they employ people in order to process a product, e.g. making motor cars, producing a person trained in a particular skill, or bringing out legislation for the good of society. Second, within each organisation, so that this process might be carried out, there are people concerned with three main tasks - handling materials, handling information, communicating with people.

As the manufacturing system grew and mass production developed, there came the demand that workers should carry out routine tasks often with little or no regard for job satisfaction or indeed for any of the needs of the individual. The incentive of pay for work was supposed to be sufficient. It is realised increasingly that routine handling of materials is actually something that can best be done by increased automation, and new skills will have to be acquired. Even during the development of the manufacturing industries a certain number of people had to be employed for the purpose of handling information. Assessment had to be made of supply and demand, systems had to be designed to fulfil these demands, deploying people as managers, salesmen and office workers like links in a manufacturing chain. Despite that, up to now our educational system has not been good at helping people to acquire the skills of communication and information processing. This inadequacy takes on a serious note when , as we have seen in Chapter 1, we note that the trend is going towards fewer jobs in the manufacturing industries and an increase in numbers in service industries where there is more concentration on handling information and on various aspects of communication.

It is the increased complexity in the process of

business, industry and government that has led to an increase in the number of people handling information. These increases are a direct result of the extension of the boundaries for business and industry from one country to operations on a world-wide scale. White, giving a summary from an international business survey, maintains that the key issues in the changing world which business and industry must address are as follows:

(1) increased political instability in many countries

(2) increasing government controls over business activities

(3) growing awareness of cultural differences between countries

(4) a growing trade protectionism in developing countries as well as in industrial markets

(5) tougher competition between countries

(6) reduction or elimination of patent and trade-mark protection by some governments

(7) increasing labour and materials costs

(8) increasing instability of currency
                    (White, 1982)

The majority of these trends can be traced to an increased communication between peoples in the various countries of the world, thus giving an increased awareness of each other´s cultural differences, business practices and methods. As a result of these trends there is a greater awareness of ecological considerations, safety for consumers and workers. There is an emphasis on the need for financial forecasting, planning and marketing techniques.

Fortunately the very methods which have led to an increased communication between countries are now helping to cope with the increased complexity and pace of change. There is, therefore, a very strong argument that we should gear our educational system to producing individuals who can both cope with the pace of change and use the methods of information technology to help them. This implies a concentration on methods of handling information and people. In view of the increase in numbers of what Strassmann calls "information workers" such concentration is essential. Strassmann indicates that in the United States information work counted in terms of hours and cost now represents more than two thirds of labour expenditure. This increase in the number of professional information workers is explained by the increasing number of managers who depend "upon the professional´s advice to cope with the increased complexity of the business environment."(Strassmann, 1985)

While pointing out that office work is the outcome not the cause of organisational design, he examines this increase in the context of office work and cites examples of the large numbers of information transactions needed in order to supply goods to a customer. In the case of government organisations who must conform to very strict regulation he indicates that "citizen requests involving even the slightest deviation from procedure can easily add up to 200 to 300 communications."(Strassmann, 1985)

When one examines the range of tasks carried out by office staff one can begin to see how the number of information handling and communication tasks can multiply so rapidly. The following gives a typical list of office workers´tasks:

Preparation

    Addressing envelopes
    Typing letters
    Preparing text
    Typing memos

The Needs and Tasks of Man

Dissemination

        Inter Office Mail
        External mailing
        Photocopying for mail
        Photocopying for local distribution
Storage

        Storing documents
        Photocopying for file

Other

        Retrieving documents
        Maintaining mail lists
        Invoicing sales ledger etc.
        Diary management
        Generating management reports etc..

                    (Adapted from Disney, 1983)

As one can see from this, many of these tasks are
virtually routine ones and are thus capable of
automation in ways already described in Chapter 2.
The implication here is thus that not only is the
complexity of the information-handling task
increasing, but because of the increased
possibilities of using the computer for routine
tasks, the concept of the office worker as someone
who merely undertakes routine information or
communication tasks will change to that of someone
who operates at a much higher level and who also
has a range of computerised equipment available.
When looking at this in terms of guidelines for
education, we must therefore recognise that, to a
certain extent, routine information tasks are being
handled in this way at present and that this trend
will increase. Since, therefore, the skills of
handling information and people are more likely to
be those already found in the ways in which
professional people operate, it is to this group
that we must look.

The tasks which professional people undertake
cannot be regarded in the same way as routine
office tasks. Professionals do not just "deal with

information", "deal with people" etc. In any analysis of the behaviour of professionals many factors must be considered. The most important of these factors are:

1. The personal factors.

>   personal background
>   home and work environment
>   job satisfaction
>   education etc.
>   maturity and self concept

Aspects of these will be taken up again later in this chapter when considering the needs of man.

2. The organisational factors.

Allen has summarised the tasks of a professional manager in an organisational context as follows:

Planning
>   forecasting
>   establishing objectives
>   programming
>   scheduling
>   budgeting
>   establishing procedures
>   developing policies

Organising
>   developing organisational structure
>   delegating
>   establishing relationships

Leading
>   decision making
>   communicating
>   motivating
>   selecting people
>   developing people

Controlling
>   establishing performance standards
>   performance measuring
>   performance evaluating

performance correcting.

(Allen,1964)

If one examines these categories carefully one can see that they are largely concerned with two basic functions, namely:

(1) processes involving information, and

(2) communication between people.

Processes involving information

Hill(1983) analyses these into five stages:

i)   input of new information
ii) retrieval of stored information
iii) manipulating the combination of the two
     above
iv) transmission of information
v)   storage of information

He cites the main sources of information for a manager as coming:

from his files, from a computer database, from the library, from his staff, from his memory.

He also quotes "Hill´s first law of information science", namely:

At least fifty per cent of the information you are given is either wrong or misleading. (Hill, 1983)

One could add to this that we receive large amounts of information which we do not need and have to seek the information which we do require. Stibic (1980) also points out that "everyone uses only the information that one can effortlessly find and ignores sources and types of information that are not easily accessible."

Thus there is a need for all individuals, not just managers, to have the right information available at the right time. The educational implications of

The Needs and Tasks of Man

this are, as Stibic puts it, the need "to learn the strategies of searching, sifting, selecting, sorting, arranging, evaluating and storing information." (Stibic, 1982)

Processes involving communication.

Communication processes can be considered as:

    (1) Contact and interaction in the organisation
      a) with those to whom he is responsible
      b) with those who work for him
      c) with others in the organisation

    (2) Contact and interaction outside the organisation
      a) with other professionals
      b) with suppliers, clients etc.

These interactions are carried out by:

    (1) Person to person contact.
      This ranges from contact with individuals to contact with groups of varying size from small committee meetings to large presentations.

    (2) Written contact.
      Letters, memos, reports etc.

    (3) Voice Contact.
      Telephone, interviews etc.

    (4) Electronic alternatives.
      Electronic mailbox, video conferencing etc.

Arising from these are additional skills summarised as skills of writing or reading; talking or listening; decision making or thinking and planning which may be needed by the individual. This examination of the external needs of man in relation to his effective performance in an organisation gives us guidelines for action in educating for the future. When looking at the tasks

The Needs and Tasks of Man

and needs of man and of society, it is necessary to begin with the individual, because, unless individuals in a group are functioning efficiently, they cannot sufficiently apply themselves to the task of maintaining the society in which they live. Let us now turn to the internal needs of man.

The internal needs.

In the following account I use Maslow´s hierarchical structure of individual needs to form a basis and background to the use of computers in assisting man to satisfy his needs and pursue his tasks in society effectively and efficiently. Maslow´s original works should be consulted if more detail is required, See, for example, "Motivation and Personality" (Maslow, 1954) or "Towards a Psychology of Being"(Maslow, 1962). A useful account of the ideas of Maslow will be found in the book by Frank Goble "The Third Force"(Goble, 1970). Maslow defines human needs in these terms:

> The human being is motivated by a number of basic needs which are species-wide, apparently unchanging, and genetic and instinctual in origin. (Maslow, 1962)

In his hierarchical structure Maslow proposes that when one set of needs are satisfied another set emerges. Foremost among these are the physiological needs, of which, need for food, liquid, air, shelter, sleep and sex are the most basic. Individuals living in civilised societies have lower needs reasonably well satisfied.

When physiological needs are satisfied the "safety" needs then emerge. These include the need for a secure base and the concept of stability which is found in most healthy adults. People who are insecure go to great lengths to avoid the strange and unexpected and have a compulsive need for order and stability. Normal people also seek order and stability, but by working from a position of security, have an interest in the new and unexpected.

53

The Needs and Tasks of Man

Maslow's next group of needs have a bearing on the performance of individuals in a group situation, the needs for love, affection and needing to "belong to". Love is defined here as Carl Rogers defines it "that of being understood and deeply accepted." People will thus strive hard for a place in a group and then strive to maintain the interactions and sense of "belonging to" that this brings.

Maslow's "esteem" needs also have relevance to group behaviour and performance as these include:

(1) Self-esteem.
    A desire for mastery,
    adequacy, achievement, confidence and
    freedom.

(2) Respect for others.
    This is important in the group context
    because it involves
    acceptance, reputation, status and
    appreciation.

After the fulfillment of basic needs by civilised society, there emerge those other needs, which relate to an individual's performance in contact with others in his working relationships and in his contact with society in general. If those needs are satisfied, then needs concerned with "self actualisation" and curiosity emerge which, if satisfied, can benefit not only the individual but also the work that he does. Self-actualisation can be defined as a need for growth and development, whereas curiosity, a need to know and understand, is a basic need for the healthy mature person. These are vitally important needs for the individual in playing his part in the maintenance and development of society.

When we consider the tasks of man in society we must see them in relation to individual needs, as both are part of the whole which, if integrated and fulfilled, will not only allow for the more effective functioning of society but will allow an individual's higher needs to emerge. This will result in him functioning at a higher level and thus benefitting the maintenance and development of society. Maslow also postulated a series of "growth" needs which emerge when people are coping well with life and which have considerable implications for the future development of societies. These include an appreciation of values as truth, justice, beauty and self sufficiency.

Thus we see that as one set of needs is satisfied and people begin to function at higher levels, so their attention begins to turn outwards and their needs embrace those larger issues of society. Maslow suggests, however, that at present only a small percentage of people are able to achieve their full potential. A consideration of this is particularly relevant at a time when the failure of business and industry in the UK to grow and develop is being blamed on the lack of risk-taking ability by management and, by implication, on the present educational system.

Maslow suggests a number of reasons why full potential is not achieved:

(1) The lower needs for safety and security constitute a strong negative influence. Growth requires a constant willingness to take chances, make mistakes and break habits. Bad habits, poor cultural environment or inadequate education can inhibit growth.

(2) Our culture emphasises controls and negative motivation rather than positive motivation. Human aspects like kindness, tenderness and sympathy are regarded as unmanly.

(3) We doubt our abilities. Maslow says, "We fear our highest possibilities... We are generally afraid to become that which we can glimpse in our most perfect moments."(Maslow, 1967)

(4) Habits are obstacles to growth. Many people tend to continue as they always have done and never examine their habit patterns. Self-knowledge and understanding are vital to growth and development. A person who is growing must constantly challenge himself and, although any new situation may generate a feeling of inadequacy, he must learn to overcome this.

Manifestations of a lack of growth can be found in many references. The acceptance that people are as they are and that it is difficult, if not impossible, to change them, is implicit in many standard texts on management. Koontz, O'Donnell, and Weihrich in their book "Management", seventh edition, writing on why people fail in planning, say:

Planning implies something new. It means change. It is well known that people resist change.

and again on management techniques:

... Managers and employees may develop patterns of thought and behaviour that are hard to change.

Managers are often frustrated in instituting a new plan simply by the unwillingness or inability of people to accept the condition of change. This is a difficult planning limitation to overcome. To do so requires patient selling of ideas, careful dissemination of information, aggressive leadership, and intentional development of a tradition of change among the members of an organisation.(Koontz et al, 1980)

In this standard reference book creative individuals who are at the higher levels of Maslow's self-actualisation process with characteristics of flexibility and curiosity are treated with some suspicion:

> Unquestionably, creative people can make
> great contributions to the enterprise. At
> the same time, however, they may also cause
> difficulties in organisations. Change as
> any manager knows, is not always popular.
> Moreover change, frequently, has
> undesirable and unexpected side effects.
> Similarly eccentric ideas, pursued
> stubbornly, may frustrate others and
> inhibit the smooth functioning of the
> organisation. Finally creative individuals
> may be disruptive to the organisation by
> ignoring established policies, rules and
> regulations. (Koontz,et al.,1980)

This latter extract seems to argue for more
bureaucratic control and less risk-taking, but to
do this stifles the very opportunities for growth
that help the individual to develop himself, and,
hence, society in general, and business and
industry in particular.

This development process may be painful not only
for the individual himself but also for the
organisation. It is, however, very necessary for
the health of that organisation.

In the past educational organisations could perhaps
justify resistance to change, since their task was
to maintain and preserve past standards for the
benefit of society. However, there has never been
any justification for a resistance to change by
business and industry, since in order to survive
such organisations need to adjust rapidly to
external conditions. A resistance to change cannot
now be justified in any type of organisation,
educational or otherwise.

5 MAN AS AN INFORMATION PROCESSOR

In the previous chapter we examined the tasks which
man is expected to carry out in playing his part in
society, and we showed in what manner, if his basic
needs are satisfied, such tasks could be carried
out more efficiently.

This chapter sets out to examine aspects of this,
since, as we have seen, these tasks are more and
more likely to involve information handling. In
particular, we shall discuss how man selects,
stores, retrieves and processes information, and
hence look at the implications for the education
process. The following chapter will build on this
to examine the computer as an extension of man.

The World of Information

The world with which we come into contact every day
consists of a tremendous array of different
objects, people and events. Bruner et al quote an
estimated seven million discriminable colours and
believe that within a few weeks we come into
contact with a large number of these.

> No two people we see have an identical
> appearance and even objects that we judge
> to be the same object over a period of
> time, change appearance from moment to
> moment with alterations in light or in the
> position of the viewer. All of these
> differences we are capable of seeing, for
> human beings have an exquisite capacity for
> making distinctions. (Bruner, Goodnow and
> Austin, 1956)

When we consider that we are receiving impressions
not only from sight, but also sound, taste, touch
and feel, we begin to see just how complex and vast

is the amount of information that comes to us through our senses.

It is important for us as educators to realise that, although it is convenient to deal with the teaching/learning process as an input/output communications model (Hills, 1986), each channel of communication is capable of holding much more than a single message, being capable of handling a vast array of subtle variations of input. Our task, as educators, is to know the possibilities and limitations of an individual's capacity to receive and process information, and, moreover, to design situations which expose students to information in such a way as to direct and focus their attention, motivating them and enabling them to remember and be changed by the experience.

Theories of Learning.

In chapter 4 of "Teaching, Learning and Communication" (Hills, 1986), I review some of the many theories of learning which abound, notably the stimulus/response theories of Watson and Thorndike; the importance of reinforcement in Skinner's work on operant conditioning and programmed learning methods; Wertheimer, Lewin and the Gestalt theory of learning. Although we need sound practical principles which can be applied to carry out the tasks defined above, very few can be distilled from the variety of learning theories which exist at present. However, the work of the more recent educational psychologists like Bruner, Rogers, Perry and Pask all reflect a concern with the student as an active processor of information and not just a passive recipient. The book of readings "How Students Learn" (Entwistle and Hounsell, 1975) provides a summary of the work of these men and a useful overview of theoretical approaches to learning appears in the book "Adult Learning" (Lovell, 1980)

Although definitive practical guidelines may be missing from present theories of learning, several dominant themes emerge. These include the need for satisfactory personality adjustment and social growth, and concern for the physical and intellectual ability of the learner. The first of these emphasises the importance of needs as portrayed in the previous chapter. Aspects of the intellectual ability of the learner are dealt with later in this chapter. Other specific guidelines which emerge are the need for motivation, the need for perception of meaningful relationships by the learner, the need to direct the learner´s attention, and the need for feedback on progress. (Hills, 1986)

Information Processing.

In the following account the possibilities and limitations of man as an information processor unaided by external means is examined under three headings:

Selecting Information

Storing and Retrieving Information

Processing Information.

The factors distilled from learning theories are dealt with under these headings. Although this account sets out to provide some guidelines for action, much more work is needed in the area of individual differences and reactions to the process of learning and of information processing. As we shall see in later chapters, it seems likely that the computer will provide the means whereby this can occur.

Selecting information.

At the beginning of this chapter we discussed the diversity of information which is reaching us every second of every day. It is impossible for us to absorb consciously more than a fraction of what is presented to us and therefore when arranging a learning situation it is necessary to ensure that attention is directed to the desired stimuli and that other stimuli are minimised or removed.

Man as an Information Processor

Directing Attention

The importance of directed attention is emphasised
by Norman as follows:

> Its remote effects are too incalculable to
> be recorded. The practical and theoretical
> life of the whole species, as well as
> individual beings, results from the
> selection which the habitual direction of
> their attention involves.
>
> Suffice it to say meanwhile that each of us
> literally chooses, by his way of attending
> to things, what sort of universe he shall
> appear to himself to inhabit. (Norman,
> 1969).

We are not consciously aware of the whole range of
stimuli reaching us. Certainly I would not know
that some millions of "discernable colours" are
seen by me "within a few weeks". I know that there
is a difference in the redness of the colour of
three books in front of me, but until I consciously
paid attention to the redness when looking for an
illustrative example I did not even consciously
recognise that three red books were within my field
of vision.

Thus, although the stimuli may be there, it is not
until we pay attention to them that they come under
any conscious control.

Broadbent proposed a "filter model" of human
information processing which begins with the
precept that, since we are only able to analyse and
identify a limited amount of information, then the
brain must act like a "selective filter" which can
be made to accept certain stimuli and reject
others. This "filter" thus reduces the load on the
processing system.(Broadbent, 1958)

Cherry´s "cocktail party problem" is a useful
example of directed attention. If we stand in a
crowded room with conversations all about us we can
direct attention to a conversation which interests

us, selecting it by filtering out to a certain extent all other sounds around us.(Cherry,1953) In this case the method we use is seemingly based on a variety of clues concerning sound quality, quality of speaker´s voices, distance, pitch, tone etc. If our ear is caught by an interesting word or phrase from another conversation, then it is possible to switch to the new conversation and filter out the old.

This direction of attention can be demonstrated by using each one of our senses. But what is the motivation that makes us want to direct attention to a specific stimulus? In the previous example it was an interesting word or phrase. The question of motivation is a central one for the teacher. How do we motivate the student and direct his attention to the message which we want him to see or hear?

Motivation

De Cecco(1968) begins his chapter on motivation with a subheading "How to increase student vim and vigor" De Cecco looks at motivation from the point of view of teacher behaviour under what he calls "the four motivational functions of the teacher ... the arousal, expectancy, incentive and disciplinary functions."

Incentive and disciplinary functions make one think of the traditional reward and punishment type of motivation, and indeed this is largely what De Cecco means when he indicates that it still occurs, although perhaps in a more subtle form.

> If the modern teacher no longer slaps
> faces, thrashes bottoms ... he still
> furrows a mean brow and grimaces when
> displeased. He may no longer string gold
> stars after the names of successful
> students but he has learnt the advantage of
> a well timed smile and a pat on the head or
> shoulder. (De Cecco, 1968)

Certainly students use a wide variety of non-verbal cues in their interactions with teachers to select what they think they should be paying attention to

and what they can safely ignore. This is perhaps
the dimension that is lacking in present packaged
learning materials and gives added weight to the
argument for using teachers as mediators of such
materials, pointing up the motivating aspect of
their role as tutors and managers of the learning
process.

Arousal and expectancy are two motivational factors
which can be related to a variety of mental and
physical factors, including personality factors,
physiological and other needs, competitive
instincts, stimulation and anxiety. Given that the
students are at a sufficient level of physiological
and other needs satisfaction (see Chapter 4) then
the motivational aspects of arousal and expectancy
can be considerable. However, whereas arousal of
interest can be motivating, such motivation can be
blocked by the arousal of anxiety, fear of
inadequacy in performance etc. It is important
therefore that a student is exposed to positive
reinforcement, - that is, he is led to expect
success, or helped in coping with a situation
however difficult, rather than always experiencing
failure and being made aware of his inadequacies.
Positive reinforcement increases the motivational
effect of arousal and expectancy.

Storing and Retrieving Information

We have seen how information to which we pay
attention has some chance of being retained. Even
so it is possible to suffer from information
overload which results essentially from being
presented with too many different stimuli competing
for attention.

Miller's article "The magical number seven, plus or
minus two: some limits on our capacity for
processing information" (Miller, 1956) cites
experiments in remembering which indicate that
there is a very strict limit on the amount of
information we can receive, store and retrieve.
Miller found that by increasing the number of
stimuli between which a person is asked to
discriminate, a limit that he called "channel
capacity" appeared where confusions began to occur.

Man as an Information Processor

This lay in the region of seven items which he called the "span of absolute judgement". Immediate memory of events also appeared to be limited by the number of items, but not their information content. Miller discussed what he called "chunking" - a process to string items together by some form of recoding or repackaging so that more items could be remembered by associating them with previously known material.

Miller makes the following observation:

> The inaccuracy of the testimony of eyewitnesses is well known in legal psychology, but the distortions are not random - they follow naturally from the particular recoding that the witness used, and the particular recoding he used depends upon his whole life history. (Miller, 1956)

In chapter 7 of "Teaching, Learning and Communication" (Hills, 1986), an experiment is described which supports this. In the experiment the people participating in a test modify their perceptions in accordance with their previous experience of the object they thought they saw. The two groups participating in the experiment were told what they would see and although the object (a crescent shape) was the same for both groups, one group tended to draw it as a moon and the other as the letter "C". Their recoding of the object was thus preconditioned to associate with previous experience. (Carmichael et al.,1932)

William James defines memory as:

> Memory proper, or secondary memory as it might be styled, is the knowledge of a former state of mind after it has already dropped from consciousness. (James, 1892)

Miller also talks of the "span of immediate memory", and is seems that for convenience sake writers on memory postulate the existence of two or more types of memory, to use James´ terms "a primary, or immediate memory" and a "secondary, or long term memory".

64

Waugh and Norman indicate that the repetition or rehearsal of items play a large part both in helping these items to remain in immediate memory and in increasing their chances of being passed to long term memory. (Waugh and Norman, 1965)

It has been found that meaningful material can be learnt more easily and retained longer than meaningless material. Material to be learnt and remembered has more chance if it can be associated with previous experiences of the learner. It would seem that one builds up "frames of reference" to which new information is related and which then stands a better chance of being remembered.

The art of improving the memory by association with known things was known to the Greeks and Romans. Cicero in "De Oratorio" tells the story of how Simonides of Ceos invented the art of memory by association, after being able to identify the remains of mangled corpses at a banquet when the roof of the banqueting hall had caved in. He did this by remembering the places in which the guests had sat.

Orators were expected to be able to deliver long speeches from memory and the basic technique suggested was to use a mnemonic place system. Frances Yates in her book "The Art of Memory" (Yates, 1966) suggests that one of the commonest was the architectural type and she reproduces a description given by Quintilian in "Institutio Oratoria":

> A series of places are formed in memory by remembering rooms and the things with which the rooms are decorated. The images by which the speech is to be remembered are then placed in imagination on the places which have been memorised in the building. This done, it is only necessary for the orator while he is making his speech, to move in imagination through the building in the correct order, drawing from the memorised places the images he has placed upon them.

65

Man as an Information Processor

That this method of association works is easy to prove for yourself at a more prosaic level by using a rhyme. First make sure that you can remember with ease the following rhyme:

> One is a bun
> Two is a shoe
> Three is a tree
> Four means a door
> Five is a hive
> Six is sticks
> Seven is heaven
> Eight is a gate

When you have this firmly in mind, take a list of objects which you want to remember, such as the following:

1. matchbox
2. watch
3. pencil
4. lamp
5. key
6. pen
7. handkerchief
8. book

Form an association with each object and a part of the rhyme. For example, "One is a bun." The first object on the list is a matchbox. Form an association between "bun" and "matchbox", then between "shoe" and "watch" and so on. It doesn't matter how the association is made, by picture or words, as long as you make sure that the association between each object and the part of the rhyme is firmly fixed in your mind before you go on to the next object. For example, the association between number 4 "lamp", and the fourth object in the rhyme, "a door", might be a picture of a lamp hanging over the door of a house.

Once you have the associations firmly in mind you can get someone to give you a number and you should be able to name correctly the object associated with this number by calling up your association.

Man as an Information Processor

This method can be extended and used in many ways. Provided that you have the rhyme firmly in your mind and take time to make associations with it, you can remember lists of things easily by this method.

In the above we have explored memory in terms of the possibilities of man's brain, but the associative method works well using only a very simple external extension of man. Having written a lecture which is to be given before a large audience, if we then pick out the main points of it, deciding on a key word for each point and then writing a list of the keywords on paper, we find that instead of reading from notes we can use the key word list to prompt us into the main points of the lecture. Frances Yates makes a telling observation on the difference between ourselves and the ancients:

> We moderns who have no memories ...
> (Yates, 1966)

Processing Information.

The brain has an ability to accept new information and to rearrange existing information to accommodate it. This rearrangement is shown in the well known series of investigations carried out by Bartlett (1932) which indicated that when subjects tried to recall stories that they had learnt their remembered versions became shorter and the language more in keeping with the subject's own vocabulary. With time there was more "constructive remembering".

We organise information into what Bartlett calls "schemata". Each new piece of information is integrated into existing schemata which are themselves changed by the new information and thus reorganised. Problem solving is therefore a process of reconciling previously unreconciled information with existing schemata in the brain. In most cases this happens slowly, but when it does happen a flash of "insight" occurs.

It is this ability of the brain to consider new

Man as an Information Processor

information and to rearrange the existing
information which it holds in order to accommodate
it that is the basis of creativity.

Creativity.

Much has been written on creativity and a number of
references are given in the bibliography to enable
you to read further, should you so wish.
Essentially creative thinking consists of knowing
the relevant facts, asking the right questions,
selecting appropriate facts and experiences, then
using the imagination, feeling and intuition as
applied to them.

Specific stages in this process are as follows:

    (1) Preparation - collecting facts and
        having experiences; asking the right
        question and defining the problem.

    (2) Incubation - leaving the problem alone
        to gel in the unconscious.
    (3) Inspiration - allowing the new idea to
        emerge into consciousness.

    (4) Elaboration - communicating the idea to
        others in the form of words, numbers,
        paint, musical notes, wood, etc.

    (5) Verification - testing the result by
        the reactions of others over time or by
        experiment. (Laytham, 1983)

This is the theory, but what of the reality?
Margolin considers the problem of blocks to
creativity and how to overcome them. You begin by
becoming aware of these blocks: "Isolating your own
fears, anxieties and hesitations helps to disrupt
those subconscious processes that distort or limit
creativity. Identifying these blocks is the first
step towards doing away with them."(Margolin, 1983)

Margolin produces a list of such blocks, as
follows:

68

Perceptual Blocks. Improper identification
or delineation of the initial problem or
gap ...Perceptual blocks involve inadequate
emphasis or focus, covering too large or
too narrow an area, as well as the
inability to see an issue from various
perspectives.

Cultural Blocks. Imposed by the society in
which you live, these blocks result from
the resistance of most cultures to change.
Based on biases and taboos, they hamper the
individual within a given society.

Environmental Blocks. Imposed by the
immediate surroundings in which you develop
your ideas, these blocks derive from
physical surroundings that are not
conducive to creative thought, eg. your
work place is too hot, too cold, too
confined, too open, or too cluttered with
too many distractions. A poor psychological
climate can be just as inhibiting (or even
more so) as in the case of ...distrustful
colleagues, lackluster competition, and
unsupportive staff.

Emotional Blocks. Personal conflicts that
arise within the individual´s own psyche.
These include the inability to tolerate
ambiguity, the tendency to judge rather
than to generate ideas, inadequate
motivation, and a broad spectrum of
self-doubts and fears.

Escape Mechanisms. Avoidance,
procrastination, diversion - turning to
another new idea before you implement the
one at hand. (Margolin, 1983)

Two of the main ways of overcoming these blocks and
promoting creativity seem to be by relaxing the
mind and changing one´s viewpoint. Margolin has
this to say on relaxing the mind:

Sometimes a certain "mental playing around"
or permitting the mind to wander and free

associate with no commitment to a fixed way
of doing things will lead to an entirely
new approach to the problem in hand.
(Margolin, 1983)

Although such relaxation is helpful, De Bono
suggests that one should also keep an eye on things
that chance puts in one´s way:

Without interfering with the chance
processes themselves it is possible to use
them deliberately by providing a suitable
setting in which they may take place and
then harvesting the results of the chance
interactions. (De Bono, 1967)

Changing one´s viewpoint is often mentioned as a
way of promoting creativity. Margolin suggests that
this can be a game:

Doing something the ´wrong´ way, just to
see what may happen, more often than not
brings into view a whole new perspective.
(Margolin, 1983)

Osborn (1963) suggests applying mental
transformation rules to a solution even if it is
unsatisfactory as it stands. Thus one can see that
by transforming it, it either becomes satisfactory
or gives further clues to a satisfactory solution.
His nine transformations are:

can it be-
    put to other uses?
    adapted?
    modified?
    magnified?
    minified?
    substituted?
    rearranged?
    reversed?
    combined?

We have seen in this chapter how man´s capacity for
storing and retrieving information within his own
brain is limited. His potential for the creative

processing of information is however considerable.
Such processing can be carried on in the brain
using external sources of information and in the
next chapter we consider some of these "extensions
of man".

6 THE EXTENSIONS OF MAN

As we have seen in the last chapter man's capacity for storing and retrieving information within his own brain is limited. Although prehistoric man must of necessity have invented a variety of ways of aiding his memory, the only aids to survive have been paintings and drawings. Knots have been used for the same purpose in many periods of history. Even today you may still tie a knot in your handkerchief, at the same time making an association with it and with something you want to remember. Herodotus reports the use of knots by the Persian King Darius. This king is said to have given instructions to the Greeks guarding a bridge to untie one knot each day and to remain guarding the bridge until all the knots had been untied. The people of Peru used an elaborate form of knots known as "quipus" which consisted of knotted cords of different colours with other cords hanging from them.

Painting and drawing, picture writing, was an important and possibly the main method of recording information before the advent of writing. Even today a traveller can make his needs understood anywhere in the world by means of signs and pictures.

Our standard pictorial road signs are another example of this. One such sign I always enjoy observing in different countries is the "man digging the road" sign. In Britain and other European countries he is generally depicted as working vigorously; but as one travels through countries where the weather is hotter so one notices that the figure sags a little more in relation to the temperature; he is depicted as not working quite so hard in the heat of the day.

At first, pictures were used to record battles, hunts and important events. The next stage in

development towards writing was the use of signs
known as "pictograms" and "ideograms". Using
pictograms the various objects making up a complex
incident were placed in a continuous sequence. The
meaning of the "sentence" could thus be deduced
from the position of the drawings. This was an
advance on the use of pictures simply for the
portraying of an incident. Ideograms gradually lost
their pictorial quality as they were intended to
represent not only objects drawn from nature, but
also ideas, actions etc. The pictorial quality was
lost because they needed to be quick and easy to
portray. The history of the development of writing
from ideogram to phonogram, from phonogram to
writing as we know it, is a fascinating study, and
references have been placed in the bibliography
should anyone wish to pursue this further (see
Mason,1920; Moorhouse,1946).

The development of writing was of paramount
importance in the presentation and maintenance of
tradition. In societies where the use of writing
was never known, the maintenance of society was
left to the composite memory of the tribe and, in
particular, to certain persons who were used as the
guardians of tribal memory.

According to tradition the people of Easter Island
met once a year to hear what was recorded in the
ancient wooden tablets which bore their
pictographic writing. These told of genealogies and
legends of the land from which their ancestors had
migrated. Understanding of them was confined to the
native royal family and a few other individuals
including priests. In 1863 Peruvian slave traders
came to Easter Island and carried off all the
leading people. Later Catholic missionaries arrived
and burnt some of the tablets because of their
pagan origin. The result was that no-one could read
what remained and the native culture of the people
was largely at an end. (Moorhouse,1946)

The survival of the Greek tradition is in sharp
contrast to this. There have been long periods of
time between our century and the ancient Greeks
when the achievements of their civilisation have
been forgotten. Yet they have not been lost, for

their achievements were preserved in writing, and, because of this, they could be read and understood afresh. Christian churches and monasteries from the start used writing for their religious and secular needs and to maintain the tradition of the pre-Christian past. They were also alive to the possibility of increasing the knowledge of the gospel by giving the power of reading to the many preliterate peoples of Europe.

The knowledge of writing, as disseminated by the Church in the Dark Ages, was not made available to the mass of the population. They received oral instruction from the priests, and for many centuries there seemed no large public need for writing. With the rise of commerce this situation began to change, since merchants found it a necessity for their business to be able to use writing. It was, however, only after the invention of printing and the consequent cheap multiplication of books that for the first time in history it became possible to bring the knowledge of reading and writing to the general mass of the people.

The invention of printing from movable type by the German craftsman Johannes Gutenberg in the fifteenth century is generally credited as heralding this mass communication and, hence, the mass storage and retrieval of information as we know it today. In fact it was only with the advent of Koenig and Bauer´s steam driven circular press, used for the first time by The Times of London in 1814 that the printed word in the form of newspapers, really began to be the agent of mass communication. At that time the press was capable of a speed of 1,100 sheets per hour. By 1865, Bullock´s roll-fed rotary press was available and this could produce 12,000 completed newspapers per hour. This speed has now been dramatically exceeded by modern presses.

The ability of man to communicate his information, knowledge of events, thoughts, ideas, actions etc. thus made a dramatic leap forward once movable type and the circular printing press had been invented. The coming of the computer has now further revolutionised the gathering and setting of information.

As a consequence there is now a variety of means of storing, retrieving and communicating information. Let us look briefly at the three established ones, those of radio, television and film. Information began to be broadcast in 1922 when the British Broadcasting Company was formed. This became an independent public corporation, the British Broadcasting Corporation, in 1927. The government had soon recognised the power of radio as a mass communication medium. Financed by licence fees, it broadcasts a mixture of news, music and feature programmes and plays. During the Second World War its home and overseas news broadcasts were of immense value as accurate sources of up-to-date information.

The coming of television reduced the amount of radio listening, especially in the evenings. As a result of this, radio began to change its image, experimenting with new programme forms, music and features for minority interests. The BBC's first television service opened from Alexandra Palace in the 1930's. The service was closed down at first in the Second World War but was later re-opened. Its revenue is (at present) derived from licence fees. Commercial television, introduced in 1954, derives its income from selling advertising time. Colour transmissions were introduced in 1967 which again influenced output considerably. There are now two BBC channels and two commercial channels in Great Britain. High definition 625-line transmission is currently used by all channels.

Both radio and television are essentially one way media which deliver information without any interaction between them and the listener or viewer. Before the advent of cheap reliable recording machines it was not possible to store and access this information. Now, however, audio-tape recorders and video-tape recorders are a common feature of many households and, although much of it is of transitory interest only, it is possible to record any or all of this information. Thus, at present, such recordings are used mainly for time displacement purposes to access the broadcast

information at a time convenient to the person
wishing to receive it.

Film is another one way medium, and it has become
polarised between epics for the large cinema screen
appealing to mass audiences and an inextricable
entanglement with television. In some cases
video-tape is being used as the recording medium to
produce films. In its pure form film is rather like
the book in that, compared with other mass
communication systems, books and films are not
regular events. A daily newspaper is a regular
event and is concerned with immediacy. Books and
films are more concerned with painting a picture of
an event on a broad canvas. They are akin to a
play, but concerned with a wider audience.

Today there are many other forms of mass
communication extending man´s capacity for giving,
storing and retrieving information. In his writing
on communications Frederick Williams cites the
following examples:

> Cable television, video cassettes, audio
> discs and video discs, video games, new
> telephones and services, personal
> computers, electronic mail and various
> types of text services....more remote from
> the public are computer time sharing
> systems (such as airline reservations), new
> digital switching networks, communication
> satellites and broad band optical fibre
> transmission systems. (Williams,1984)

These are all manifestations of the coming together
of developments in computers, telecommunications
and advanced electronic circuitry. What this means
is that man has gradually extended his means of
processing, storing, retrieving and communicating
information from the verbal communication of the
local tribe to the market-place of the world. There
are two other aspects of the electronic revolution
which should be considered: on the one hand the
"information circling the globe within seconds"
aspect, and the other very personal and individual
aspect to the generation of information, the
interaction between individuals and the computer.

The Extensions of Man

The computer is the ultimate extension of man, at the moment. At whatever period one is writing one is apt to write of the ultimate which the future then extends. In the case of the computer, it is capable of such flexibility and possible future development that it is difficult at the present time to think that it will not play the major part in man's future existence and destiny.

McLaughlin in an article entitled "Human Evolution in the Age of the Intelligent Machine" (McLaughlin,1983) suggests that machines should become dominant on Earth within 100 years through the continued development of existing man-machine systems. This conclusion will be considered again in Chapter 9, but the point to be noted here is that computers are potentially the nearest and most intimate extension of man since the invention of pen and ink.

This book has been written on sheets of white paper with a fountain pen containing black ink. The pen has been an extension of myself. I have set down facts, thoughts, ideas and conclusions which follow from the basic framework that I have set for the chapters. To use my writing as an extension of myself I have decided on the approach, the subject matter, the scope, the intended audience and the level of treatment. I have sought more information on aspects of topics where I am lacking in knowledge. I have used and transformed that information for my purposes and then shaped it into publishable form to be communicated to and used by others. This is a very personal process which occurs between me, my pen, and the paper on which I write. It is a very personal process because I can shape, edit, rewrite, change, transpose and perform any number of operations on what I have written before writing a final draft.

The ordinary typewriter can be used in a similar way, but it is not as flexible and rapid as the pen. It is designed essentially to produce line after line of text and this interferes with the freedom of the nonlinear process of thinking, writing and shaping.

The computer on the other hand is quite different. Although it can imitate a typewriter it can do much more than it. It can be used to store, edit, change, and transpose ideas and information. The final drafts of this manuscript were, in fact, composed on a BBC Model B Microcomputer using "Wordwise".

The Triune Brain Theory.

Chapter 2 has shown us some of the things of which the computer is capable and has indicated some of the things that it may be capable of in the future. The computer is so special because it is akin to the brain of man. It is, or can be, literally an extension of the brain of man. Paul Maclean, Chief of the Laboratory of Brain Evolution and Behaviour at the National Institute of Mental Health in Bethesda, Maryland, USA, some years ago proposed a "Triune brain theory" which enables us to see the computer as a possible extension of man.

His triune brain theory suggests basically that in its evolution the human forebrain has expanded to great size while retaining the basic feature of three formations that reflect our ancestral relationship to reptiles, early mammals and recent mammals. These three formations constitute a hierarchy of three brains in one, each building on the functions of the other, but retaining some of the features of the other. This theory has a wide currency and will be found, for example, in Koestler´s "Janus: a summing up",(Koestler, 1978) and in "The Dragons of Eden" (Sagan,1977). As Maclean himself says, the theory is useful in "getting a handle on" something as unmanageable as the brain. More than this, it shows how nature, rather than disregarding and starting again, develops and fashions from whatever it has.

Now, as with many things, man has taken a hand in a process which nature began and is hastening its development.

The Extensions of Man

Maclean in his article "Education and the Brain" says we:

> are all part of nature, everything that we
> do must be considered natural.
> Nevertheless, if we read nature correctly
> ... then perhaps we can speed up the
> process .... Perhaps it is time to take a
> fresh look at ourselves and try again to
> act accordingly. (Maclean, 1978)

Carl Sagan begins his book "The Dragons of Eden" by saying:

> Our children will be difficult to raise,
> but their capacity for new learning will
> greatly enhance the chances of survival of
> the human species. In addition, human
> beings have, in the most recent few tens of
> a percent of our existence, invented not
> only extra genetic but also extra somatic
> knowledge: information stored outside our
> bodies, of which writing is the most
> notable example. (Sagan, 1977)

Now of course the computer is beginning to be the most notable example. This invention extends the possibility of our knowledge store far beyond that commonly thought possible only a few years ago.

The Fourth Brain.

The computer can be thought of as man's "fourth brain" (Hills,1985), taking its place alongside the other three in Maclean's theory. Maclean says:

> In its evolution the human brain expands
> along the lines of three basic patterns
> which can be characterised both
> anatomically and biochemically as
> reptilian, paleomammalian and neomammalian.
> Radically different in their chemistry and
> structure and in an evolutionary sense
> countless generations apart, the three
> basic formations constitute, so as to

> speak, three brains in one or, more
> succinctly, a triune brain. What this
> implies is that we are obliged to look at
> ourselves and our world through the eyes of
> three quite different mentalities ....
> Moreover, it should be emphasised that
> despite their extensive interconnections
> each brain type is capable of operating
> somewhat independently. (Maclean, 1978)

Thus there is the realisation that even within our
present brain, "each brain type is capable of
operating somewhat independently" and, even with
the addition of our external "fourth brain", should
continue to do so. Indeed viewed in this way the
addition of the computer to the reptilian,
paleomammalian and neomammalian brains, adds yet
another set of dimensions to man´s potential for
creative thought.

The electronic computer as man´s fourth brain
offers a tremendous potential for fast and accurate
recall of data, whereas the other three, which can
be thought of as comprising man´s biocomputer,
possess immense flexibility and adaptibility.

The present position would seem to be that the
fourth brain stores, processes, receives and
retrieves information which the biocomputer then
adapts for human tasks and needs. This is, however,
too simplistic, for electronic computers can and
are being built to be more powerful and, with
developments in artificial intelligence and expert
systems, are becoming more flexible and capable of
undertaking what at present we could call low level
thinking/processing. These developments are bound
to continue to develop much further.

What of the human biocomputers? It is clear that
these come in a variety of shapes and sizes. What
is not yet clear (the nature/nurture debate) is
whether it is merely faulty programming on the one
hand and more effective programming on the other
that creates the differences in different human
biocomputers (Hills,1982). Because the computer
can interact like, as it were, a fourth brain, it

will be increasingly possible to explore the human
biocomputer in terms of the electronic one.

The concept of a machine as an extension of man is
not new. Indeed Asimov´s robots were the
forerunners of the reality of today where robot
arms and other automated devices are in common use
with some manufacturing processes. The concept of a
machine as an extension of man´s brain appears in
an article by Vannevar Bush in The   Atlantic
Monthly, July-December 1945. In this article
entitled "As We May Think", Bush, the then Director
of the Office of Scientific Research and
Development in America, who co-ordinated the
activities of thousands of leading American
scientists in the application of science to
warfare, urged that scientists should turn from
extending man´s physical powers to extending the
powers of the mind. He contrasted the human brain
with what he called "the artificiality of
indexing". Data stored in a library is filed
alphabetically or numerically and is retrieved by
tracing it from sub-class to sub-class. Unless
duplicates are used, it can only be in one place
and the rules used to find it are cumbersome. The
human mind, however, he went on to say: "operates
by association. With one item in its grasp, it
snaps instantly to the next that is suggested by
the association of thoughts, in accordance with
some intricate web of trails carried by the cells
of the brain." He qualifies this by admitting that
some trails are prone to fade and some items are
not permanent "memory is transitory. Yet the speed
of action, the intricacy of the trails, the detail
of mental pictures, is awe-inspiring."

Although he felt that man could not fully duplicate
this process artificially (how much nearer are we
some 40 years afterwards?) he suggested a device
which could act as an, albeit limited, storage and
retrieval system. He gave it the name "Memex". His
original description follows:

> A memex is a device in which an individual
> stores his books, records and
> communications, and which is mechanised so
> that it may be consulted with exceeding

> speed and flexibility. It is an enlarged
> intimate supplement to his memory. (Bush,
> 1945)

In 1970 Bush in his autobiography commented:

> No memex could have been built when that
> article appeared. In the quarter-century
> since then, the idea has been with me
> almost constantly, and I have watched new
> developments in electronics, physics,
> chemistry and logic to see how they might
> help to bring it to reality. That day is
> not yet here, but has come far closer.
> (Bush, 1970)

Although his descriptions are in terms of the device
available to him in the 1940's, his thoughts and ideas
much to inform us on the possibilities for the computer
the extension of man. Take, for example, his summary
the way some professionals might use the trai
established in the memex:

> The lawyer has at his touch the associated
> opinions and decisions of his whole
> experience, and of the experience of
> friends and authorities. The patent
> attorney has on call the millions of issued
> patents with familiar trails to every point
> of his client's interest. The physician,
> puzzled by a patient's reactions, strikes
> the trail established in studying an
> earlier similar case, and runs rapidly
> through analagous case histories ...(Bush,
> 1945)

In 1986 these "trails" exist, lawyers do have a
legal computer database available to them, work is
going on with expert systems that can diagnose a
patient's illness through an analysis of their
symptoms. However, these things are still piecemeal
and experimental. They do not yet use the computer
in the completely flexible and interactive way they
will when the computer can be fully regarded as
man's fourth brain; that day, however, is I am
convinced not far off.

Even if the computer has yet to become the fourth brain, it is being seen as an "independent personality" and a companion, as many people who work with computers will know.

> Certainly each different system I "talk" to is a separate identity.

> When a program does something I have taught it to do, I am pleased in much the same way, perhaps, as I would be if I had taught a person to do such things.

> Another described the computer as a "friendly helper", but added a qualification: "That depends on the computer. I would never call a TRS-80 a friend of mine." (Marvin and Winter,1983)

In this same account the process of transaction with the computer is described in quotations from a variety of users as follows:

> I pull the strings, but it has a pair of scissors.

> Sometimes it´s the classic pain of dealing with an over-literal child, and cursing your flawed efforts to communicate with it.

> (Some) computer systems constantly refuse to trust their users. They are programmed to act as if they always know what is best, and what is right and will not consider changing their minds. Just like outside bureaucrats. So I don´t use those systems if I can help it.(Marvin and Winter, 1983)

The Ultimate Extension of Self.

What are the consequences of the computer as man´s fourth brain, the ultimate extension of self? Certainly as we have seen the computer can give man a "super power memory" and through developments in expert systems help him to process the stored information, match it against incoming information, manipulate data and make rapid decisions.

This sort of use considers the computer as a "stand-alone" device, interacting with the brain of man, but as we have seen one of the advantages of computers is that they can be networked, linked together and can interact with each other. Thus we have a situation which is potentially akin to the concept of the "universal mind" which can be tapped by anyone who has a "mind" to do it. This brings in a whole host of questions about data protection, privacy of the individual, confidentiality of information etc. We are just beginning to take our first steps in data protection with the Data Protection Act, but many people seem not to be worried by such considerations. The implications of a "universal mind" may, however, be even more far reaching than many people realise at the present time. Although some people appear to be able to empathise with others, that is they can project themselves so as to understand the feeling of others, and man is essentially a gregarious species, he is also a solitary one. No-one can tap into his innermost thoughts - yet! These and other related points are discussed further in Chapter 9.

7 INFORMATION TECHNOLOGY AND EDUCATION

We have investigated in the previous chapter the
limitations and possibilities of man as an
information processor/learner and seen how the
computer can interact with him to offset the
limitations and extend these possibilities. The
computer and the methods of information technology
are being applied to and are being used in
education in a variety of ways. The simplest form
of introducing the computer to the classroom has
been to teach computer literacy, keyboard skills
and simple programming, and to make use of it for
simple tasks. Teachers adopting this somewhat
cautious approach have often found themselves
overtaken by some students who by using their own
home computers have gone beyond this.

Teachers have also found the computer extremely
valuable as an aid to visual demonstration, as,
given the limitations of the screen size and the
definition, it is possible to prepare still and
animated demonstrations on it for use in the
classroom situation. These uses are, however,
examples of how a new technology is often at first
treated in a traditional way. The excitement and
the challenge of the computer and the methods of
information technology are such that they cannot be
contained by the traditional ways of education.
Computers are a potential extension of the self,
and as such cry out for "hands-on" experience. This
is well evidenced by observing a class of students
working with computers, by the popularity of home
computers and by the work of projects like the
Microelectronics Education Programme. Although
this project ended on 31st of March 1986 (See
"MEP: the Final Byte", Fothergill,1986), a
Microelectronics Support Unit will continue to
exist. Another project which sees microcomputers
and new technology as central to its philosophy is

the "Education 2000" project based in Letchworth. A short introduction to this project appeared in The Times 11th March 1986 as "Teachers get Training for Classrooms of the Future" (Hodges,1986). Papert's book "Mind Storms" (Papert, 1980) is a very readable account of the creative way in which young children work with computers.

Educational Technology

Because computers interact directly with the learner they fit well into an educational technology perspective of education, defined as follows:

> Educational technology is basically the application of a systematic or systems approach to education. Such an approach is often seen in terms of three aspects
>
> (1) the specification of the educational objectives of a course
> (2) the determination of the teaching/learning methods to be used, and
> (3) the evaluation of course material in terms of the objectives set for it.
> (Hills, 1982)

Thus educational technology and information technology (as defined in the introduction to this book) come together to form what is potentially an infinitely powerful system of use for educational purposes.

The Interactive Element

Chapter 3 of "Teaching, Learning and Communication" (Hills,1986) explores the variety of methods, techniques and resources available to the teacher. The essential difference between the microcomputer and other methods is that prior to the existence of the microcomputer, the teacher had a variety of resources at his command, - books, radio, television etc., but largely had to supply the

interactive element himself. If we take just one of
the resources, broadcast television programmes, as
an example, we can find that as well as being
intended for entertainment, they often contain
educational aspects. Some documentary programmes
are particularly good, especially the ones which
deal with nature and the things about us.
Television is a medium which can be described as
very attention-engaging, for it can present a wide
range of sounds and images from anywhere in the
world brought together in a unique combination to
illustrate specific aspects of a subject. In
educational terms there are dangers in this,
especially when portraying political events or
human issues. Bias and the portrayal of only one
side of a picture are obvious dangers. Some
television producers will justify this by arguing
that they are only concerned with "good television"
or "entertainment". If teachers want to use such
material which is, perhaps of necessity,
unbalanced, it is necessary for them to use several
sources which together will give a more balanced
picture.

Video recorders have, of course, brought with them
the advantage of being able to repeat broadcast
television at times of one´s own choosing both in
school and in the home. There are videotapes now
available for sale or hire on a growing range of
educational topics. Although these are largely
non-interactive, the teacher can use them to extend
his own store of images and enhance his teaching.
In this way he thus supplies the interactive
element which is so necessary in the teaching/
learning process. Present television programmes,
however excellent and motivating, are only a
one-way medium. They assume that there is a passive
audience sitting watching and listening. In this
they are similar to the one teacher talking to a
large class, but the use of colour, the moving
images, etc., obviously enhance the process in a
way that is not easy for a teacher in routine
teaching. In spite of this, the teacher still has
to supply the interactive element.

Sound radio, like television, is a once only
one-way medium and unless recorded is not

repeatable. Books, on the other hand, can be read more than once, can be picked up and put down when convenient, flicked through, randomly accessed etc., all of which are features which help to involve the student. For an amusing , yet accurate, summary of the advantages of books as an educational method, one should read "Learn with Book" (Heathorn, 1981).

The advent of the computer has brought with it a new dimension. It is itself capable of providing an interactive environment in which the student can be guided through sequences of instruction, provided with remedial sequences depending on his response to key questions etc. It can, once programmed correctly, replace the teacher in certain situations. The variety of methods and techniques which now exist all centre around the use of the computer, either by the student using its interactive features directly, or by it being used in combination with one or more other media to form an interactive learning environment with the teacher as manager, mediator and tutor. When used as a computer with just the usual additional devices, keyboard, screen, storage system and primer, although it can be flexible and interactive in helping students to learn, it is limited in the quality of the graphics and it cannot generate pictures of photographic quality. Interactive video, however, gives the computer the facility to present moving and still pictures of photographic quality and to superimpose text and graphics on them. Although not necessary for every situation and at the moment relatively expensive for general use in schools, nevertheless the potential is there.

When it comes down to it, the present reality, however, is that present computer programmes do not take advantage of their flexible interactive possibilities and have largely followed what might be called the traditional teaching mode, that is, a linear teaching mode with some branching, using multiple choice questions reminiscent of the linear and branched programmed learning sequences of the 60´s.

Information Technology and Education

The computer is capable of a much more complex level of student interaction, for it can provide information on student errors and it can tailor sequences at different levels of difficulty for the student, depending on his responses to key questions. With flexible scheduling it allows students to work on the computer at convenient times and at their own pace. It can also impose a time limit for answering questions or completing sequences if desired. It offers immediate knowledge of the results of tests and can offer remedial sequences to correct errors. Used as an individual learning device it can both motivate the student and, an important feature in view of an earlier comment about students´ fear of exposing themselves to criticism in discussion, it offers the advantage that students can make mistakes which the machine merely treats neutrally and helps them to correct. Hence it can help the student to build his confidence without fear of exposing his mistakes to others.

At the moment the computer is largely a teacher mediated device and as such is capable of providing a student with self-instruction which can be extended and co-ordinated by the teacher. The computer´s potential to link with a variety of data-bases and to text and video picture sources means that teachers of all subjects can enrich students´ learning experience considerably. The use of simulations and games, very familiar in education and training, can be extended by the computer. It can be used to present simulations of virtually any situation, its use as a flight simulator being a particularly well known example. It is especially useful for simulating dangerous experiments or potentially dangerous real life situations. It has the tremendous advantage of immediate feedback and so can accept instructions, show how they affect the situation being simulated and then be ready to accept another set of values if the first did not produce the desired result. Obviously in flight simulation when faulty handling means that the plane crashes, or in the simulation of a medical diagnosis where the "patient" dies, such computer simulation offers considerable advantages over other more conventional methods!

Meeting the Increased Demands for Education.

To date these increased demands have been catered for by a variety of methods including distance learning and open learning, and by organisations and initiatives like the Open University and now Open Tech.

We have already seen the increased demands on education both from a wide variety of organisations and individuals and for a range of educational needs, often outside that of the formal educational system. These include:

> Young adults who failed in the school system but want to take up their education again without going back to school.

> Adults who by virtue of the demands of their work cannot find the time to attend traditional classes but who require retraining. It has been estimated that many employees will require retraining every 5-10 years to do what is essentially the same job.

> Mothers with babies or young children who want to continue their studies.

> People on board oil rigs, in remote locations, or in prison who want to take professional courses leading to certification.

Open Learning is the current term used to cover the variety of present initiatives which have arisen to cater for the educational needs of the groups described above. Open Learning, essentially, uses the methods of educational technology and with no clear distinction between it and "Distance learning", the name probably stems from the methods first used by the Open University and now widely followed by other initiatives across the world.

Open Tech. is a recent Manpower Services Commission

initiative which was briefly described in the previous chapter.

"Open Learning" is a convenient term to use and is generally taken to mean the following:

> It is a system of learning or training that allows individuals to tackle their chosen subject in a place, and at a pace that suits them best.
>
> The "place" might be home, work or a college or industrial training location, or even on the bus! The "pace" may be hours, days or weeks. These factors allow for personal or employment commitments or any other barriers which may stand in the way of on-going education or training.
>
> Open Learning programmes or packages consist of workbooks, audio or video tapes, computer programmes, practical kits, and combinations of any of these, depending on the subject. (Midtech, 1986)

Open Learning thus uses the methods of educational technology and is now beginning to embrace the use of information technology.

Open Learning could be regarded as the forward battleground for computer learning, since all of the problems which have arisen in connection with open learning and the control and use of materials by teaching staff are arising in the use of computer based materials. Many of these lessons have been learnt from projects like "Midtech" which is an open learning delivery system , offering a range of packaged learning materials to increase educational and training opportunities for adults in Bedfordshire, Cambridgeshire, Hertfordshire, and Milton Keynes. There are a number of developments like Midtech throughout the country working with the Open Tech. programme, and although the majority of materials available at present are paper-based, the use of computer programmes is increasing and will take more advantage of their interactive facilities than is at present the case.

91

The major problems in colleges of further and higher education have been associated with staff use of materials. In a recent review many factors were found, ranging from lack of appreciation by Heads of Departments in seeing the potential uses of such materials, the impossibility of finding the money to pay tutors properly to administer the range of open learning materials needed to fulfill student needs in an institution, to union problems where staff refuse to allow students the use of open learning materials without staff supervision. (Hills,1985a)

This latter problem is exactly akin to the problems arising in automating factory processes where some unions are trying to insist that the automated machines are supervised by the operators of the previous generation of machines.

Although these problems will continue, eventually both the methods of distance and open learning will be accepted and the increasing use of the computer to cater for the needs of the groups mentioned above will greatly improve the learning potential of these systems through the creation of interactive learning environments.

There is also the implication, already recognised in open and distance learning systems, that the computer, used as an interactive learning environment and linked via a modem to the telephone line forms a communication channel that theoretically allows that learning environment to be extended to, and used, anywhere in the world. It certainly extends education beyond the physical bounds of the school, college or university into the home, office, remote community, etc., etc.

The micro-computer also possesses an advantage that has been noted when comparing television with traditional teaching, namely the facility of concentrating the attention. Material presented in such a relatively small area as a television screen concentrates student attention wonderfully and may increase the rate of assimilation of the material. One necessary condition for this is that the material presented is clear and easily assimilated (Hills, 1986).

The Student´s Viewpoint.

In students´ eyes, traditional school teaching techniques suffer badly in comparison with the presentation of educational material on television and the interactive use of computers. Additionally some students are discouraged by the mixed classes of the comprehensive school with their inability to cater for the vast range of individual differences and backgrounds of students in a single class. Present use of computers in schools, although often patterned on traditional teaching, is demonstrating much improvement in student motivation and if used in the fully interactive mode should both improve the rate of acquisition of knowledge and students´ attitudes to their work.

The interactive nature of the system is such that not only can student errors be corrected the moment they are made, but students can also be shown why they made such errors. Further information or instruction can be given when the preceeding information has been assessed by the computer as having been assimilated by the student. The student proceeds at his own rate; brighter or more advanced students can proceed at a higher level of difficulty than those whose rate of assimilation is slower, or those whose background knowledge is deficient. The point has already been made that the machine is a patient, ever present, neutral object helping, not intruding with human characteristics.

The Teacher´s Viewpoint

Teachers, however one defines their role, whatever their job description and whatever the detailed content of the syllabi they communicate to their pupils, have taken on the task of educating our future generations. They do not have a full and proper description of how to do this and no-one at the present time is completely in a position to help them.

Rather than encourage and help them, all that society, the government, industry, the professions, etc. etc. seem to do is to blame them for not doing their job. But what is their job? - no one knows completely. Many teachers therefore prefer not to think about what they are doing but simply to "get on with the job" which to them is "teaching" a set syllabus to groups of students in a set time for a written examination. That is not good enough. Teachers are hard pressed and, in my opinion, do not get sufficient monetary reward for their efforts, but perhaps part of their efforts lacks the focus that it should have. The use of microcomputers in schools adds yet another dimension for the teacher to be concerned with. They may see the introduction of micro-computers as a threat to replace them by automating the educational process. The true situation is that microcomputers can actually help teachers to achieve this task by removing from them many of the dull, routine, repetitive tasks in which they are forced to engage at present, thus leaving them time to stand back from their tasks to think about their role and the role of education in society. The present task is thus to rethink the role of the teacher and the structure of the school, thoughts which are developed in the next section.

One of the major boring and largely repetitive set of tasks is concerned with the correcting of exercises, entering the marks on to a mark sheet, adding them to existing marks and producing class averages, class orders etc, etc. This is a task that the microcomputer can do supremely well. With the use of a variety of self-test techniques student answers can be recorded by the machine and a variety of calculations performed on the ensuing marks. Not only can work be marked, but, what is very important, immediate feedback can supply an explanation of errors, thus using them positively to promote and accelerate learning.

The teacher is thus manager of the process and at present, although the microcomputer can, with suitable programming, be a fully interactive learning environment, it is not capable of helping reasoning skills. The teacher thus decides on the overall direction and mix of subject material and uses a combination of methods and sources of material to maintain interest and motivation in the pupil. It is questionable even when much more progress has been made with artificial intelligence and expert systems applied to education whether a total diet of sitting in front of a screen all day would be desirable when one of the major purposes of education at present is to facilitate interaction with others.

The Organisational Viewpoint.

In a manufacturing process one looks at a variety of factors which have the ultimate objective of selling as many objects as possible at as high a price as possible. In order to seek optimum production techniques one examines factors such as:

what the public wants

how much it will buy and at what price

how cheaply and easily the desired object can be made

how best to publicise, market and sell it.

In the educational process we are not dealing with a standard manufactured product. Although earlier we defined the aims of education in terms of benefit to the individual and to society, this does not give us the complete answer. Are we trying to impart knowledge, alter attitudes (what are students' attitudes in the first place and how are they formed?), are we trying to achieve flexibility of mind, stimulate creativity etc., etc.?

The immediate answer is that we are trying to do this and more. But how? There is no clear link between what we as teachers do and what happens at the student end. Nor indeed is there any definitive guidance on what processes we should apply to produce a clear cut result at the student end. There is certainly no clear directive in present

There is certainly no clear directive in present teacher training courses, or indeed any clear indication of increased "productivity" from teachers who are more highly qualified by certificate or diploma than others.

The efficiency of the system is now being called into question by the rising costs of education and by the inability of the educational system to meet the present demands on it. There is no longer justification for any educational organisation to teach a merely subject-based curriculum or simply to provide narrow job-related training. The task of education is to educate for a society in which careers change; there is a need for retraining; there will be more unemployment; there will be more self-employment, more job-sharing, more leisure opportunities. The challenge is to educate for self-direction and development in the individual, to promote a questing, creative, positive attitude to life rather what can be best represented as a passive attitude of unquestioning acceptance of what passes for media entertainment at the present time.

Traditional school systems were geared to the training of an elite, ie. the passage of the more able student from grammar school to university and into the professions. They have not adapted well to a situation which is mass education in the sense of catering for a variety of levels and types of pupil with a diversity of career opportunities and prospects. Perhaps the reason is that, although the system has adapted to mixed classes, the basic teaching methods and philosophy of most teachers have not adapted. Teachers still largely teach in the same way and whereas "normal" classroom teaching was to an extent successful with a relatively narrow spread of type of pupil and ability, it is not effective in the mixed ability classes of today.

Such traditional teacher-centred class teaching contrasts sharply with the possibilities offered by the change in the teacher's role to encompass the use of the microcomputer and the variety of resource and learning materials available, both

through the use of the computer and in addition to
it. These new methods can both motivate and
interest the students and cope with their
individual differences.

There is, from the point of view of the traditional
teacher, a much more serious problem posed by the
microcomputer and associated devices, namely that
education need no longer be confined to schools.
Open learning and distance learning through
viewdata, teletext and interactive video allied to
paper-based materials, with self-help through
electronic networks are all becoming accessible to
individuals. All of these methods mean that
students can study in a variety of situations
outside the formal system, scheduling courses to
fit within their own time commitments. The
implications for education are tremendous, the
"threat"(if it is seen as that) to the traditional
system is enormous. The possibilities for the
teacher to play a leading role in the changes and
to expand his role are considerable. This
possibility is considered further in Chapter 8.

8 THE TEACHER´S ROLE IN PLANNING FOR THE FUTURE

In the previous chapters we have looked at the background to the present socio-economic electronic revolution in which we find ourselves. We have seen what the computer can do, how it and developments in telecommunications can be regarded as immensely powerful extensions of man. We have surveyed the present changes in education and in the last chapter have examined implications of the new technology for education as far as we can see it at this moment. But what of the future? The only thing that we can be certain of is that change will continue and that we and our future generations must be able to manage and control that change for the positive benefit of mankind.

In planning for the future the task before us is to develop a perspective which will enable us to anticipate change and to manage it in order to produce a healthy and flourishing society. This should then be followed by communicating this perspective to our children to help them to understand and learn techniques which, using our own tentative beginnings, will enable them to make the creative leaps of insight necessary for planning and guiding the future of mankind.

John Christopher Jones, looking at it from the perspective of the designer, has this to say of the present situation and the way it is developing:

> Perhaps the most obvious sign that we need better methods of designing and planning is the existence in industrial countries of massive unsolved problems that have been created by the use of man-made things eg. traffic congestion, parking problems, road accidents, airport congestion, airport

noise, urban decay, shortage of such
services as medical treatment, mass
education and crime detection. (Jones,
1981)

Although writing in the context of design, his
arguments are very relevant to the wider context of
human communication and education, and consequently
we shall examine them in that light. His
proposition is that there are several levels which
should be considered:

The lowest at the level of components; for
example, rooms in houses, car engines, etc.

The next is at the products level; for
example, houses themselves, vehicles
containing engines.

A third is the systems level; housing,
traffic etc.

I maintain that the formal education system can be
considered as an example of this third level.

Jones states that these are the levels at which
designers usually operate at present, but that
there is a fourth level which is concerned with the
relationships between systems. In the extract
quoted above we can see that this would embrace
traffic congestion, parking problems, road
accidents etc. All this he calls the "community
level".

At this fourth level aspects of user behaviour,
social and political implications relevant to
relationships between systems must be considered.
The problem with things like traffic congestion and
parking problems is that they appear at the systems
level but they are not entirely within the province
of, and cannot be put right by central or local
government or by those who suffer the problems.
They can only be solved by a combined attack. As
Jones puts it, there is a need for foresight
combined with organised planning so that "the
developing systems can flourish in concert rather

than multiply in confusion." (Jones, 1981)

Although writing a decade earlier and on the
subject of "The Roots of Violence and Vandalism",
Mia Kellner Pringle makes essentially the same
point:

> In the past thirty years, a revolution has
> been brought about in the health and
> physical development of children by
> applying new medical and scientific
> measures. In the next thirty years, a
> similar revolution could, I believe, be
> brought about in their mental health by
> applying new social, psychological and
> educational knowledge....
>
> ... with regard to means, no one
> professional group or government department
> - local or central - has the key. Health,
> housing, social and educational measures
> must all combine to seek solutions to
> poverty and multiple deprivation. What is
> needed is a kind of inter-professional
> combined operation. (Pringle, 1973)

If one considers things in this light the first
premise is that in planning the future we are not
just looking at the formal education system, the
health service, the social services, the political
system, unemployment, prevention of crime and
violence, the young, the aged, the family and the
child. We are concerned with "the community". In
essence we are dealing with human communication,
aspects of interaction between people and people,
aspects of interaction between people and systems,
and aspects of interaction between people and the
developing use of machines. How then can we
approach and explore these interactions? Not, I
would suggest, by an increase in restrictive
control by government and other agencies, but by
more participation, by more public and professional
awareness of these systems, more thinking about
systems and especially about their actions and
interactions. What is needed as Pringle says is "a
kind of inter-professional combined operation".

The Teacher´s Role in Planning for the Future

I believe that it is up to us as educators to
initiate and maintain this combined operation and
that it is timely for us to do this. Teachers are
by the nature of their training, inclination and
activities, both able to conduct research, collect
and weigh evidence, weld it into a coherent and
balanced account and put it across to others. By
now well used to "action research" in their own
classrooms, this would be action research in the
"real" world where teachers meet with other
professionals to produce an interdisciplinary
approach to the problem. We have already seen and
commented that the one essential feature of our
future existence will be change and that the only
stability is centred in the individual who will
have both to initiate , cope with and control
change. The future will thus be shaped by the level
of needs by which individuals are operating, by
their beliefs, their ideas and their values. Our
concern as educators is to explore this complexity
of values, needs, beliefs and concepts, and to
adapt or redesign our educational system to promote
the development of the individual for stability and
for a changing but secure future.

To undertake such a task is a radically new step
for teachers. We are used to being subjected to a
period of training which fits us to be teachers,
and teachers we become. Teaching is perhaps the one
profession where the basic methods and way of
training have changed little in the last fifty
years. There is now a much greater emphasis on
in-service training, but this is usually taken to
be subject-based in-service training. As we have
indicated in a previous chapter, it is the
insistence on keeping rigid subject divisions that
is likely to hold up the development of education
for today´s needs and tomorrow´s world.

What we are advocating here is basically the
development of a "self-directing teacher" approach,
where the teacher sees himself as someone who goes
out of the classroom, to meet and interact with
other professionals. He does this to examine and
help to solve the problems which are thrown up at
the community level of society. These results are
then taken back to the classroom so that they may

be communicated to the next generation.

Written in the context of the deprived child, but equally true of the development of any child Mia Pringle says:

> a variety of strategies will have to be
> explored for promoting optimal emotional
> and intellectual development ... and, most
> difficult of all, for breaking into the
> vicious circle of the emotionally and
> intellectually deprived children of today
> becoming tomorrow´s parents of yet another
> generation of deprived children.
> (Pringle,1973)

We have already noted the swing of employment from manufacturing physical goods to service industries and Stonier´s comment that only 10% of the population will be required for physical manufacturing. If Stonier is correct, or even approximately correct, these levels of securing our future need not be considered to be at risk. It is at the level of systems and human interactions that we need to think of the future.

How then can we begin to tackle the problem? We should first of all examine previous attempts by teachers to promote change, particularly in the area of curriculum developments. Once having done that we should all carefully specify the task and establish what guidelines are available for tackling it.

Teachers and Curriculum Change

Although teachers have an extensive background of experience in attempting to change both what they teach and to influence the curriculum and its evaluation, it is salutary to examine it in the light of what is being proposed above. Crossley refers to the 1950´s and to the 1960´s as the time when we "discovered" curriculum development.

> Characteristically for these buoyant times,
> curriculum innovation tended to be
> ambitious, and large in scale ...... the

> centralised research-development-diffusion
> model of curriculum change was widely
> adopted ....
>
> In retrospect, however, despite
> considerable success in terms of syllabus
> and materials development (and adoption),
> the large scale centre-periphery approach
> to innovation is now widely acknowledged to
> have generated little substantial change in
> terms of educational practice. (Crossley,
> 1984)

When looked at broadly one finds that such
experience is amply confirmed from other evidence,
for example, Herron, 1980; Kelly, 1970 etc..)
Unfortunately, it seems that as a whole the variety
of methods and techniques used to effect change in
teaching have been largely unsuccessful in creating
the full extent of the changes hoped for. This does
not mean to say that researchers and writers are
not still hopeful. Many strategies and methods of
inducing change have been and are still being put
forward. David Whitehead's book "The Dissemination
of Educational Innovations in Britain"
(Whitehead,1980) is a useful summary of evidence
and ideas in this area, and other sources include
the method of "Organisational Development" (Taylor,
1981). This has been described as "the most active
school of thought that has emerged which provides
theory, research and practical thrusts for
institution-wide efforts" (Dalin and Rust,1983).
Nicholls(1983) provides a useful summary of issues
and problems of innovations, including their
introduction and maintenance, in his book "Managing
Educational Innovations".

The conclusions of most attempts to influence the
teacher and change the curriculum, certainly at
school level, are perhaps best summarised by
Whitehead as follows:

> (1) Teachers will not voluntarily take up
>   innovations and use them in the way in
>   which the originators intended unless
>   there is systematic dissemination built

into a project.

(2) Desired changes in teachers´ approaches should be brought about by means of induction courses and training programmes.

(3) No project is likely to succeed unless it takes into account possible motives on the part of the teacher adopting it (eg. beneficial effect on teacher´s status, promotion prospects, or earnings).

(4) Local teacher meetings are helpful in encouraging the cross-fertilisation of ideas. These must be in work-time and must be perceived to be of practical utility.

(5) This necessitates commitment of the local authority to the innovation, and the provision of facilities for the release of teachers for inservice (re-) training. (Whitehead,1980)

Whitehead sees teachers mainly as the recipients of innovation, not the initiators. Obviously in most curriculum development projects a certain number of teachers have been involved in the development of techniques, methods and materials to a greater or lesser extent. The number who could be involved centrally have always to be strictly limited, the rest being recipients. The vast majority have therefore had to accept the findings of the research and then been expected to adapt and adopt the resource materials in a local context.

The present situation calls for a different strategy. Rather than a few educationalists seeking an overall countrywide solution and then hoping to impose it on the rest, we are now concerned with a much more fundamental problem which is the concern of every teacher and calls for a "bottom-up" approach rather than a "top-down" one. Enough evidence exists today to show that the important

The Teacher's Role in Planning for the Future

aspect in the spread of any educational innovation is a consideration of the human interactions. The knowledge and resource materials to tackle the problem exist to help teachers in their task, but the thrust must come from those very teachers working in a local context. From local initiatives and from resulting networks which can and are being created general principles will emerge. These can be refined both to tackle the present problems of society and to use in training for future generations. The important point is that the knowledge, if it exists, is fragmented between many people in different disciplines and between many published sources both in subject and in time. The equivalence between the writings of a designer and someone who was formerly Director of the National Children's Bureau serves to illustrate this point.

Lessons must be learnt from previous attempts at educational innovation and change and the main ones of these are perhaps best summarised by Nicholls who lists the following difficulties encounted in implementing innovations:

(1) Many educational innovations require considerable changes in teachers' attitudes, for example in team teaching teachers move from the privacy of a "self-contained classroom" to teach in the presence of colleagues.

(2) An innovation frequently requires teachers to give up practices in which they feel secure and display high levels of competence and adopt new practices in which at least temporarily they feel less secure.

(3) The extra work and time load that planning and implementing innovations bring are in addition to normal teaching duties and should not be overlooked.

(4) The cost of innovations is also often cited as a difficulty.
(Nicholls, 1983)

105

The Teacher's Role in Planning for the Future

Adams and Chen on the other hand neatly summarise the main factors associated with the process of innovation:

(1) Innovations usually fail.

(2) Barriers to innovation invariably emerge.

(3) Resistance to change seems universal.

(4) Change is usually transitory.

(5) Willingness to change appears related to conditions in society.

(6) Change may or may not be rational.
(Adams and Chen, 1981)

Without careful consideration of these factors, without the enthusiasm of teachers and their realisation that the proposed change is not only vital to the future of society but also vital to their own role in that society, and without the backing of education authorities and government agencies, none of these factors could operate. However, conditions are right at this moment. The variety of present initiatives outlined in Chapter 3 show that there is an increased awareness of the need. Let us therefore begin to define the task in more detail.

The Chinese have a saying that a journey begins with but a single step. The process by which we must proceed is very like the teacher as explorer, looking for hidden treasure in an unknown land. Progress is made by making a "network" of journeys.

This network (of journeys) is not something that exists before he begins, he has to invent it, either before he starts or as he proceeds.(The difficulty) is that of coping with the complexity of a hugh search space filled with millions of alternative

combinations of possible sub-components.
(Jones, 1981)

Mager in his seahorse fable was concerned with
defining the objectives of education:

> If you're not sure where you are going, you
> may well end up some place else.(Mager,
> 1962)

Thus, a careful statement of the task as far as it
is known at the moment will help to begin the
journey , but it must be born in mind that the
journey itself may well provide information which
will subsequently modify the objectives. However,
unless we have them to begin with, there is no
indication of where the journey should start nor
what route it should follow. Setting objectives for
the search has much in common with educational
objectives as described by De Cecco in the
following terms:

> The teacher must determine at the start
> what the student will be able to do at the
> finish. A careful statement of this
> terminal behaviour enables the teacher to
> plan the steps the student must take to
> achieve it.

Looking at it from the student's point of view he
continues:

> If the student knows beforehand what he
> must learn in any given unit of
> instruction, he can better direct his own
> attention and efforts. (De Cecco,1968)

The Task.

We must realise that the teaching profession is in
danger of turning in on itself. This attitude of
teachers behaving as though the classroom is apart
from the realities of a changing world is
compounded by a number of factors, not the least of

these being those given in Chapter 1 (page 9). It
is the responsibility of teachers to grasp this
situation, to explore it further and act
accordingly.

The Need

I think it of paramount importance that teachers
ought and need:

> (1) to be in touch with the changing world,
> with aspects of leisure, work and society
> in general.

> (2) to have a repertoire of methods
> appropriate to the role of teacher as
> manager, mediator and tutor.

> (3) to realise that the development of the
> individual is the key to change and
> therefore that their role is to help the
> individual learn how to learn and to
> promote his skills of thinking and
> creativity.

Methods for the dissemination of innovation like
the centre-periphery model have been largely
unsuccessful. The need, therefore, is for teachers
to engage in action research and become more
involved in industrial, community, environmental
and educational aspects of society throughout their
local area. In planning the future we should not
just be looking at fragments of the whole: the
formal education system, the health service, the
social services, the political system, unemployment, prevention of crime and violence, the young,
the aged, the family and the child. We are
concerned with "the community". The essence of this
is human communication, interactions between people
and other people, people and systems, people and
the increasing use of machines.

There is an urgent need to examine the changing
ways in which we as individuals are affected by
these interactions. We need to examine the
implications of this now and for the future, both

for this generation and the generations to come. We need to explore its dimensions in social, environmental and educational terms, and apply our findings to the educational system.

It is important to see that the computer and its allied developments have begun both to accelerate the rate of change of our society and to offer certain solutions to this change. Where these solutions lead depends on how man responds to them and appreciates their implications. The next chapter considers some of the aspects of this in "The Computer: Master or Servant?" In the final chapter there is a summary of some guidelines and pointers to the future needs of education and to the teachers´ role in providing this.

9 THE COMPUTER: MASTER OR SERVANT

Computers are taking over many of the tasks of man.
In some industries indeed the automation of
materials handling is well advanced. Moreover, it
is well known that the routine information handling tasks of office workers can be more effectively
and efficiently handled by computers and allied
devices. Because of the increase in the complexity
of the tasks of business and industry this trend is
bound to grow and will continue to grow. In
addition, computers will be increasingly used for
more complex tasks involving decision making.
Expert systems are being developed and a variety of
artificial intelligence applications, which can be
used for higher level tasks, is being investigated.
Computers are still at a stage where they are the
servant, yet even now it is possible that they
could be seen as posing certain threats to mankind.
What "dangers" lie ahead, and what is the essential
difference between computers and humans?

From the beginning the computer has excelled in
performing complex calculations rapidly and
efficiently. With the advent of silicon chip
technology the cost, speed and power of computers
has increased. In Chapter 2 there is a review of
the components and associated devices which go to
make up modern computers and we note how present
systems and networks link these devices together so
that information, numerical data, text, pictures
and graphics can be rapidly accessed anywhere in
the world. In all of these applications the
computer can be seen as making man more powerful.

Adele Fasick, writing in the context of the North
American educational scene, sees the development of
the wired information society as posing a
considerable threat to future educational systems
if these depend on computers and other
communication devices based in the home:

> While middle-class families may be able and
> willing to provide abundant communication
> devices for their children, poor families
> will become relatively even more deprived
> than they are now. The larger the
> investment required for participating in
> the information society, the wider the gap
> between the rich and the poor will become.
> (Fasick,1984)

As Fasick points out, the situation is more complex
than simply a question of money, for at present
parents often do not have sufficient awareness of
the importance and possible future effects of
computers in the education of their children. Some
of these possibilities are further outlined in an
article "Children and Electronic Text: challenges
and opportunities of the new literacy." (Paisley
and Chen,1982)

Possibly because of a general lack of appreciation
of the present and future possibilities of
computers many people see them as a potential
threat to the quality of life. As Steve Shirley
says:

> The computer regulates uniformity by
> imposing the average, the confirmist and
> the banal...Variation lies at the root of
> our genetic survival and has created our
> human individuality. In manufacturing
> environments, managers foresee product
> perfection in the faultless repetition of
> the computer. However, the very absence of
> elective variation eradicates the
> possibility of exceptional excellence as
> well as the possibility of disaster.
> (Shirley, 1984)

This is not just a consequence of the introduction
of computers, for, as we saw in Chapter 4,
pre-computer era thinking seems actively to have
discouraged individuality, exceptional excellence
and creativity.

Creative individuals may be disruptive to

111

the organisation by ignoring established
policies, rules and regulations." (Koontz
et al., 1980)

The nature of man is towards growth and creativity
and we need such excellence, innovation and
creativity for the survival and growth of our
society. Shirley sums up what many people feel at
present when she says:

> Most people resent being treated as clones
> with identical product needs, identical
> performance capacities and possessing
> judgement inferior to a machine. They
> resent an assessment of their worth based
> on their ability to understand computers
> and to co-operate with the computer's
> primitive communication capacity. (Shirley,
> 1984)

These largely instinctive fears about computers may
be well founded, for implicit in them is the fact
that, although the computer is servant to those
rich and powerful enough to afford it, it could be
seen as yet another master for those who suffer its
effects and who are not in a position to protect
themselves. This brings into question aspects of
the privacy and protection of individuals since
almost daily we are giving some piece of personal
information to a bank, an insurance company, a
government agency etc., etc. As Lindop points out:

> We know nothing of how that information is
> handled, stored or used; we have to hope
> that our intrinsic vulnerability to the
> misuse of such information will not be
> exploited. In particular we have to assume
> that the only data which is held about us
> is correct, the minimum necessary, and will
> not be put to uses other than those for
> which we first provided it, or given to
> other people or other information systems,
> without our consent. (Lindop, 1983)

On the 12th July 1984 the Data Protection Act
received Royal Assent and passed on to the statute

book. It is the first piece of legislation in the United Kingdom to address the use of computers. The purpose of it is to protect information about individuals and to enforce a set of standards for the processing of such information. The following information about the Act is taken from the booklet "The Data Protection Act 1984. Guideline No.1. An Introduction and Guide to the Act." (Office of the Data Protection Registrar,1985)

The Data Protection Act meets two concerns. The first is that arising from the threat which mis-use of the power of computing equipment might pose to individuals. This concern derives from the ability of computing systems to store vast amounts of data, to manipulate data at high speed and, with associated communication systems, to give access to data from locations far from the site where the data are stored. The second is that arising from the possibility of damage to our international trade which might occur if the United Kingdom were not to ratify the "Council of Europe Convention for the Protection of Individuals with regard to Automatic Processing of Personal Data." Countries ratifying this Convention might place restrictions on the transfer of personal data to countries which have not ratified it.

It is important to note that the Act is

> to regulate the use of automatically
> processed information relating to
> individuals and the provision of services
> in respect of such information.

The Act does not therefore cover the processing of personal data by manual methods. Nor does it cover information relating to corporate bodies. It does lay down certain definitions, the following of which are part:

Personal data consists of information about a living individual, including expressions of opinion about him or her, but excluding any indication of the intentions of the Data User in respect of that individual.

<u>Data Users</u> are organisations or individuals who control the contents of personal data processed, or intended to be processed, automatically.

For more details of the definitions or further information about the Act, the Act itself should be consulted (HMSO, 1984), or the booklets listed under "The Data Protection Registrar" in the bibliography should be consulted.

The 11th May 1986 was set as a deadline after which it is an offence to hold personal data without being registered as a Data User (unless entitled to an exemption) or to provide bureau services without being registered as a Computer Bureau. It is also an offence to operate knowingly or recklessly outside the terms of the registration entry made. This is an important step forward, because, while it does not entirely remove the threat of the use of computers in a "master" situation, it does indicate some measure of responsibility and control. As Cherry (1985) pointed out, information about us is recorded anyway, but the important point is that it is not available in one place. The important point about computers is that they are capable of collecting it in one place and that place is then potentially available worldwide for many unspecified purposes.

The computer is different from any other device we have so far experienced in the development of the civilised world. It is different because it is akin to the brain of man, or the brain of man is akin to it. The description of it in Chapter 6 as man´s "fourth brain" taking its place alongside the "three" brains of man, as postulated by MacLean, recognises that the brain can be regarded as a biological computer. Lilley has said that:

> All human beings, all persons who reach
> adulthood in the world today, are
> programmed biocomputers. No one of us can
> escape our own nature as programmable
> entities. Literally, each of us may be our
> programs, nothing more, nothing less.
> (Lilley, 1974)

114

So far in our development the brain of man has been largely a closed system. By that I mean that no-one has been able to access man's personal thoughts and feelings unless he has wanted them to, when he expresses these by word or deed. However, it is becoming increasingly apparent that such methods of accessing man's innermost thoughts do claim to exist, namely "telepathy","thought reading" and other "extra-sensory" methods which may well be based on an unconscious analysis of peripheral cues. Man is actually externalising his internal thoughts all the time by word and deed but, depending on the situation and the amount of control exerted by an individual, the clues to these inner thoughts may be so small as to be undetectable to another individual under normal circumstances.

Lie detectors are an example of picking up involuntary physical responses which then show differences between responses for truthful statements and untruthful ones. Nor is it just a physical response. Lie detectors now exist which analyse spoken utterances, changes of tone and pitch, in order to establish the truth or otherwise of answers to questions. In the same way that the voice can be analysed to determine if an individual is lying, so it is possible that a complete analysis of the content of an individual's speech and conversation in a variety of situations could yield many clues to his innermost thoughts, emotions and motivating influences. Seen in a positive way this could lead, for example, to a more accurate diagnosis of his state of health. Seen in a threatening way such an analysis could provide the means of obtaining even greater control over the individual, thus providing the means for the manipulation of the thoughts and actions of individuals or groups. Such manipulation could range from influencing their purchasing habits to the way in which they interact and react with others.

These are dangers which are with us now and are occasioned by our present uses and thoughts about computers. Since much of the present argument and

115

thought about the future use of computers centres on the difference between man and the computer, what is the essential humanness of human beings?

Cherry listed the distinct characteristics of human behaviour as being "choice, purpose, intent, meaning and other cognitive activities". He considered that computers:

> do not possess the higher powers of ab-
> straction, central to the process of
> understanding, which would require, in
> addition, abilities to create universals,
> hypotheses.(Cherry, 1985)

Testing such understanding and intelligence was the subject of Turing's well known test of machine intelligence "The Imitation Game". This required a human interrogator to ask questions of a human and of a machine contestant, judging their "humaness" from their written replies.

McLaughlin has said that:"it is not necessary that the machine really cognate like a human, only that it be smart enough to simulate the appearance of that process." (McLaughlin, 1983). Results from Turing's test would thus be misleading if the machine were successful. In any event it is likely to produce a misleading impression of computer intelligence. The classic fear behind testing a computer for human behaviour is the fear that it may become dominant over human beings. McLaughlin suggests that such comparisons are ill-founded since "the two organisms will not share enough in common to provoke a meaningful conflict."

McLaughlin writing on "Human Evolution in the Age of the Intelligent Machine" was concerned that there was a relative lack of integration between the components of man's brain, making him a "weak evolutionary contestant" as compared to the development of intelligent machines. He considered that machines should become dominant on Earth within the next 100 years as a result of the development of existing man-machine systems. In particular he hypothesised the emergence of a

"hyborg", defined as: "an intelligent machine or
network of such machines which has incorporated
humans into it as dependant components much in the
way that the present human brain has subsumed the
brains of lower life forms."

He continued:

> it would be naive to assume that the germs
> of these hyborgs can be accurately
> identified today, but certainly some
> candidates can be discerned in the fields
> of electronic games and entertainment,
> prosthetic medicine, communications,
> banking, automated education and the
> military. The last choice, if dominant in
> the system, might well be a lethal
> mutation. (McLaughlin,1983)

Implicit in this last statement is the problem of
Mager´s seahorse.

As we have seen, developments in educational
technology are accelerating the rate of change of
our society and creating a number of problems
associated with increased communication between
peoples of the world. The same technology is
offering us "solutions", but since, as McLaughlin
points out, computers are capable of developing in
ways that are neither discernable nor
understandable by human beings at the present time,
we cannot be certain where these "solutions" will
lead. Before totally rejecting McLaughlin´s
hypothesis, however, it is salutary to reflect on
the classical paradox of who is the servant and who
the master!

10 EDUCATING FOR A COMPUTER AGE

Although the formal education system is in the middle of a period of considerable change, teachers, while beset by a complexity of educational initiatives, changing courses and examinations, pre-vocational training etc., are still for the most part teaching subject-based syllabuses in traditional ways. The profession is also struggling with its own identity, its professionalism and the endless saga of trying to achieve parity of pay with other professions. If one adds to this the influence of the new technologies we meet in every aspect of our lives, the new methods, media and techniques that can and are being applied to education, the needs for adult training and retraining, the interest that many organisations are showing in their own educational needs, one begins to get some idea of the complexity of the present situation. These facts in themselves constitute pressures which would daunt any normal profession.

Teachers, if they have time to think about this, realise that they have two main alternatives. Either they can go on teaching in the way in which they have always done and hope that the problems outside the classroom will go away or that things will settle down to their previous steady state, or they can hope that they will be able to do something about the situation in which they find themselves. They could, of course, leave teaching, but this would be to depart from the field, and teachers, in my experience, are for the most part born optimists and stayers.

There is no point in hoping that teaching will ever be what it was before, a leisurely profession which imparted information on a number of set subjects, preparing students for examinations which led to the professions and training those who fell by the wayside in other ways for less skilled jobs which required less in the way of thinking skills. Even the ways of the traditional teacher have now been eroded and outmoded, for classes of mixed ability cannot be taught effectively by the traditional classroom method.

All of this combines to create a situation in which teachers have lost a secure base and the concept of security that, as we have seen in Chapter 4, is so necessary for the proper functioning of the healthy adult. This is not a situation, I may add, of the teachers´ making. In addition to everything else, circumstances have shaped the situation in such a way that there is little true understanding among the general public of the teacher´s plight and the real needs of the educational system. To put it simply, but in a way that reflects the basic problem, it seems impossible that anyone is going to help the teachers unless they help themselves. Indeed, since teachers are the people best placed to appreciate the full significance of what is happening in education, this means that they must rise up from the present situation, take on all comers and reaffirm in the strongest possible ethical way the presence of their profession.

Teachers must do this for the survival both of our present and our coming generations. For this, parents should also come into the teacher´s special consideration. For example, as Fasick reminds us, at present parents do not have sufficient awareness of the importance and possible future effects of computers. There is, however, a problem even greater than this, because in our present rapidly changing world, if we count only the waking hours of our students, although teachers take about one third of these for their contact time, it is the parents who have the remaining two thirds as potential contact time with their children. To ensure that students get the maximum exposure and guidance in working towards the future, it is therefore necessary for teachers to consider how to give help and guidance to the parents so that they may both be prepared for and make sense of the present situation.

For the word "parent" one can substitute "adult" or "individual", since it is not only in their role as parents that they need guidance in a world of ever increasing complexity. The complexity of life has increased considerably - an individual has to cope with an increasing number of regulations, forms and transactions. Organisations have to design procedures to cope with the increasing complexity of handling people and information. We have to bear in mind that routine procedures are being increasingly handled by computers but, as Strassmann(1985) indicates: "citizen requests involving even the slightest deviation from procedure can easily add up to 200 to 300 communications."

We must constantly remember that teaching is the one profession in the world that is concerned with the development of the individual in the context of a developing society. The only thing we can be certain of in the uncertain age in which we live is that change will continue and that we and our future generations must manage and control that change for the positive benefit of mankind. All of this adds up to an important message for all educators:

> There is a vital job of education and
> re-education to be done for our present and
> future generations, for young children,
> students and adults. Other professionals
> and other organisations outside the present
> formal education system show an interest in
> the parts of the problem that interest them
> but it is only the teacher, potentially at
> least, who is in a position to set the
> whole in a balanced perspective.

In order to carry out this awe-inspiring task teachers must assume the role of researcher, disseminator of information, and manager of the learning process. The present situation needs to be explored by looking at: the formal education system, the health service, the social services, the political system, unemployment, prevention of crime and violence, the young, the aged, the family and the child. We are concerned with "the

120

community". In essence we are dealing with human communication, aspects of interaction between people and people, aspects of interaction between people and systems, and aspects of interaction between people and the developing use of machines. These dimensions of tremendous importance to mankind need to be explored in social, environmental, industrial, economic and educational terms. Because the results of all this are of importance to all, the results should be communicated by the most appropriate methods and techniques we can find to do this.

As we have said, to undertake such a task will be a radically new step for teachers. Up until now we have been accustomed to being subjected to a period of training which fits us to be teachers, and teachers we become. Teaching is perhaps the one profession where the basic methods and ways of training have changed little in the last fifty years. Teachers are, however, by the nature of their training, inclination and activities, able to carry out such research, collect and weigh evidence, weld it into a coherent and balanced account and disseminate it to others.

Where to begin?

In Chapter 8 we defined the problem and looked at the task before us, but the big question is where one should begin when, as Jones says:

> coping with the complexity of a high search
> space filled with millions of alternative
> combinations of possible sub-components?
> (Jones, 1981)

All research must begin with one or more hypotheses to indicate at least the direction and purport of some preliminary journeys into the unknown. What are our present guesses for educating for a computer age? The following account extracts some of these indications given in previous chapters.

Let us begin with the overall concept of education, since the decreasing opportunities for employment, the need for higher skills and the increase in time to do other things all pose considerable problems for the individual. We must switch the individual's concept of education from seeing it as something simply to fit him for employment. Indeed it is vital for him to regard it as a preparation for life, a concept which educators have long held as an ideal but which now must become a reality. It must become a reality in a world where people interact much more with computers, where work is no longer necessarily in one place and can be based in the home with computer links to a central organisation. All of this helps to contribute to less person-to-person contact with consequent individual factors of social isolation. Personal contact with others is an essential pre-requisite of the human condition. This brings us to one essential hypothesis mentioned earlier, namely that human beings are essentially gregarious creatures. Only by mixing with and talking to others can they completely maintain mental health and a balanced personal perspective of the world in which they live.

We must consider a host of such needs as proposed in Maslow's hierarchical structure of individual needs as when one set of needs are satisfied, another set emerges. We have noted how the emergence of higher needs can benefit the maintenance of society. Our journeys should include a consideration of ways of development of the individual so that the higher needs and an appreciation of truth, justice, beauty and self-sufficiency can emerge. This may be thought of as a highly generalised statement of an unattainable ideal, but in a computer age we are perhaps closer to a means of achieving this ideal than we have ever been.

Computers are taking over many of the tasks of man. The automation of materials-handling is well advanced in some industries . Thus the opportunity exists to use computers and robots in order to free people from the routine task of life and work, to give them more time to think, to develop and exercise creativity and higher thinking skills so that the appreciation of such ideals can emerge. We have seen how at present there is some ambivalence about the efficient running of business organisations and the need for creativity and innovation. There is no question that the nature of man is ever towards growth and creativity and that we need such excellence, innovation and creativity for the survival and growth of our society. Hence, however painful creativity and innovative thinking may be in the routine functioning of organisations, strategies must be developed by which organisations can cope with this, if they are to thrive. There is general agreement that we must educate ourselves, our colleagues and other educationalists for a greater appreciation of the processes of wealth creation and the place of industry in the maintenance of society. We must also educate industrialists and others to give them a greater appreciation of the worth of creative and innovative minds and the methods of education appropriate to developing them.

The use of robots, computers and other automated devices for low level routine tasks throws into sharp focus one major hypothesis about our future educational system, namely that it should be concerned with promoting understanding about interactions between people and people, people and systems, and people and machines. As we have seen earlier, these translate into concern with life skills and communication skills. The growing realisation of the importance of these aspects is echoed by many educational organisations and examining boards from which the following examples have been chosen.

In the formal school system, the Schools Curriculum Development Council were concerned with, amongst others:

Personal and social education, including the preparation of pupils for adult life.

Communication Skills... in relation to pupils´ conceptual development and their need to express increasingly complex ideas to a variety of audiences.

and in the further education sector, the Further
Education Unit´s concerns included:

An ability to develop satisfactory personal
relationships with others

A basis on which the young person acquires
a set of moral values applicable to issues
in contemporary society

Sufficient political and economic literacy
to understand the social environment and
participate in it

An appreciation of the physical and
technological environments, and the
relationship between these and the needs of
man in general and working life in
particular

A flexibility of attitude and willingness
to learn sufficiently to cope with future
changes in technology and career.
(FEU,1982)

There is in fact no shortage of such statements
emerging in a variety of contexts across the total
educational spectrum. The awareness of the need is
there. However, the process of educational
innovation goes broadly from a recognition of the
problem and statements of intent such as those
above to syllabuses, courses and examinations which
give further detail. From these there is a natural
progression to teaching and/or learning materials
for the student. Syllabuses, courses and
examinations reflecting the types of concern
expressed above have been emerging in the past few
years but often in the context of the
"disadvantaged", the "less-able", those with
"special needs". We seem to have a knack of hitting
on exactly what is needed and then instead of
applying it to the mainstream of our education,
relegating it to the sidelines. This is not to deny
the importance of the sidelines, but there is also
a considerable central need for these as well. We
need to recognise and implement this now.

Educating for a Computer Age

In seeking guidance for the most appropriate ways of putting information across to students and helping them to develop and learn, we have noted that the few definitive guidelines which exist can be expressed in terms of motivation, the direction of attention, the need to make the material relate to that which has been previously known to the student, and the need to give feedback on progress. The micro-computer can, with proper programming, supply all of these needs.

When we looked at the way the brain functions we saw particularly that the brain has an ability to accept new information and to rearrange existing information to accomodate it. Each new piece of information is integrated into existing schema which are themselves changed by the new information and re-organised. Problem solving is thus a process of reconciling previously unreconciled information with existing schema in the brain, and it is then that "insight" can occur. It is this insight that Cherry(1985), as cited in an earlier chapter and worth the mention again, points to being the essential humaness of human beings: "choice, purpose, intent, meaning and other cognitive activities and ...the higher powers of abstraction, central to the process of understanding."

This is why the microcomputer, used to store, retrieve, present, and interact with the brain of man, adopts the features of both to the best advantage. Bush(1945) saw this in his description of the Memex and the human brain which he saw as operating:

> by association. With one item in its grasp,
> it snaps instantly to the next that is
> suggested by the association of thoughts,
> in accordance with some intricate web of
> trails carried by the cells of the brain.

There is no question that computers can be made to simulate human intelligence. Sophisticated decision making programmes and artificial intelligence applications which do not need a human brain as a mediator are being developed now for use

125

with existing computers. In business, financial, military and other applications, where the results may be the important thing, it may not matter that the computer is not working in tandem with the human brain. In education, however, since our concern is to promote human learning, we are concerned with a dual operation, the computer acting as an extension of man to help him develop his cognitive processes.

Changing teacher roles and behaviour patterns will not be easy. Adams and Chen(1981) have given us the somewhat dismal conclusions that innovations usually fail and that there are barriers to innovation and change. These are all related to the present teacher attitude and behaviour. Nicholls (1983) however, has argued that such negative attitudes are engendered in teachers due to a reluctance "to give up practices in which they feel secure and display high levels of competence."

Whitehead(1980) pointed out that very human motives were involved such as the "beneficial effect on teachers´ status, promotion prospects and earnings" and recognised at the same time the importance of LEA backing and the provision of facilities as vital to such change. It is vital that educators overcome these barriers and negative attitudes. Many of them result from factors such as those given by Maslow and discussed previously. These are concerned with the need for safety and security, a culture which emphasises controls and negative motivation, doubts about our own abilities and habits as obstacles to growth.(See page 55) They need to be tackled and beaten. Maslow sums it up as:

> Growth requires a constant willingness to take chances, make mistakes and break habits. (Maslow,1962)

Teachers are there to promote growth. Teachers have always been there to set an example. Let us all strive to carry this out now.

BIBLIOGRAPHY

Adams,R.S.and Chen,D. (1981) The Process of Educational
    Innovation: an international perspective.Kogan Page,
    London/Unesco, Paris
Allen,L.A. (1964) The Management Profession. McGraw-Hill,
    New York
Asimov,I. (1953) The Second Foundation. Doubleday & Co.,
    New York.

Baker,K. (1983) Foreword to The Information Technology
    Yearbook 1983/84. (P.J.Hills & R.Martlew,eds.) Century
    Publishing, London.
Bartlett,F.C. (1932) Remembering. Cambridge University
    Press, Cambridge.
Broadbent,D.E. (1958) Perception and Communication.
    Pergamon Press, Oxford.
Bruner,J.S.,Goodnow,J.J. and Austin,G.A. (1956) A Study of
    Thinking. John Wiley, New York.
BTEC, (1984) A Policy for the 1990's BTEC, London.
Bush,V. (1945). "As We May Think".The Atlantic Monthly.
    176. July-December 1945. pp.101-8
Bush,V. (1970) Pieces of the Action. Morrow, New York.

Carmichael,L., Hogan,H.P., and Waters, A. (1932) "An
    Experimental Study of the Effect of Language and the
    Reproduction of Visually Perceived Form".
    Journal of Experimental Psychology. 15. 73.
CBURC, (1983) Computer Facilities for Teaching in
    Universities. A Report by the Computer Board for
    Universities and Research Councils. London.
Chandler,G. (1986) "Industry Year. Reviewing a Century's
    Decline".Link-Up. Jan.- March 13-16
Cherry,C. (1985) Information Technology and Social
    Revolution (Compiled and edited by William Edmondson)
    Croom Helm, London.

Bibliography

Crossley,M. (1984) "The Role and Limitations of
   Small-Scale Initiatives in Educational Innovation".
   Perspectives No.4 533-40.

Dalin,P.and Rust,V. (1983). Can Schools Learn?
   NFER-Nelson,Windsor.
Data Protection Registrar (1985) The Guideline Series.
   No.1. An Introduction to the Act. Office of the Data
   Protection Registrar, Cheshire.
Data Protection Registrar (1985) Questions and Answers on
   the Act. Notes to help you apply for registration.
   Office of the Data Protection Registrar,Cheshire.
De Bono, E.(1967) The Use of Lateral Thinking. Jonathan
   Cape,London.
De Cecco,J.P. (1968) The Psychology of Learning and
   Instruction. Prentice-Hall Inc., New Jersey.
DES. (1985) The Development of Higher Education into the
   1990's. Cmnd 9524. HMSO. London.
Disney,C. (1983) Towards the Electronic Office. Further
   Education Unit, London.
Duffy,M. (1984) "Education 2000?"Science and Public
   Policy. 11. 6. 365-8.
Durham,K. (1984) "Society's Demands on Higher
   Education."International Conference of Higher
   Education, University of York
Dutton,P.,Nicholls,P.,and Presst,B. (1984) All Change.
   National Extension College, Cambridge.

Entwistle,N. and Hounsell,D. (1975). How Students Learn:
   implications for research into post-compulsory
   education. University of Lancaster.

Fasick,A. (1984) "Education Policy and the Communication
   Gap". Science and Public Policy. 11.6. 384-5
FEU, (1982) A Basis for Choice, 2nd.ed. Further Education
   Unit, London.
FEU, (1984)Information Technology in Further Education
   Further Education Unit, London.
Fothergill,R. (1986) "MEP: the Final Byte". Times
   Educational Supplement 21 March 1986. p.9.

Goble,F.G. (1970) The Third Force. Grossman Publishers
   Inc. New York.

Bibliography

Heathorn,R.J. (1981) "Learn with Book" in The Future of
   the Printed Word (P.J.Hills ed.) Open University Press.
   Milton Keynes. p.171.
Herron,J. (1980) Quoted in The Dissemination of
   Educational Innovations in Britain (Whitehead,D.J.)
   Hodder and Stoughton, London.
Hill,M.W. (1983) "Information for Middle Management
   Decision Making". Paper given to Annual Conference of
   F.I.D. 1983
Hills,P.J. (1982) "Educational Technology" in A
   Dictionary of Education (P.J.Hills,ed.) Routledge and
   Kegan Paul, London.
Hills,P.J. (1985) "Human Communication: Through Knowledge
   to Wisdom.Interdisciplinary Science Reviews. Sept.1985.
Hills,P.J. (1985a) "The Experimental Authorities Project".
   Unpublished Report to Bedfordshire LEA
Hills,P.J. (1986) Teaching, Learning and Communication.
   Croom Helm, London.
HMSO (1963) Report of a Committee on Higher Education
   under the chairmanship of Lord Robbins.
HMSO (1984) The Data Protection Act. HMSO   London.
HMSO (1985) GCSE. The National Criteria. Department of
   Education and Science, Welsh Office. HMSO. London.
Hodges,L. (1986) "Teachers get Training for the Classrooms
   of the Future".The Times 11 March 1986.

James,W. (1892) Psychology. Henry Holt,New York.
Jones,J.C.(1981) Design Methods: the seeds of human
   futures. John Wiley, London

Kelly,P.J. (1970) "The Process of Curriculum Innovation"
   p.84-104
Koestler,A. (1978) Janus: a summing up. Hutchinson.
   London.
Koontz,H.,O'Donnell,C.,Weihrich,H.(1980) Management.
   7th.Ed. McGraw-Hill,New York.

Laytham, G. (1983) Notes on Creative Thinking. (Personal
   Correspondence)
Lilley,J.C. (1974) The Human Biocomputer Sphere Books,
   London
Lindop,N.(1983) "Data Privacy". in The Information
   Technology Yearbook 1983/84. (P.J.Hills and
   R.Martlew,eds.) pp.213-17. Century Publishing, London.
Lovell,R.B. (1980) Adult Learning. Croom Helm, London

Bibliography

Maclean,P. (1978) A Mind of Three Minds. Educating the
    Triune Brain. In "Education and the Brain" pp.308-42
    77th.Yearbook of the National Society for the Study of
    Education. University of Chicago, Illinois.
Mager,R.F. (1962) Preparing Objectives for Programmed
    Instruction. Fearson Publishers, California.
Margolin,J.B. (1983) The Individual's Guide to Grants.
    Plenum Press, New York.
Marvin,C.,and Winter,M. (1983) "Computer-Ease: a twentieth
    century literacy emergent"Journal of Communication. 16,
    33. 92-108
Maslow,A.H. (1954) Motivation and Personality. Harper and
    Row, New York.
Maslow,A.H. (1962) Towards a Psychology of Being. Van
    Norstrand, New York
Mason,W.A. (1920) A History of the Art of Writing
McHale,J. (1976) The Changing Information Environment.
    West View Press, Colorado.
McLaughlin,W.I. (1983) "Human Evolution in the Age of the
    Intelligent Machine". Interdisciplinary Science Review.
    8. 4. 307-19
Midtech (1986) Midtech Open Learning: Introduction.Midtech
    Open Learning Unit, Letchworth.
Miller,George A. (1956) "The magical number seven, plus or
    minus two: some limits on our capacity for processing
    information". Psychological Review. 63. 81-97.
Moorhouse,A.C. (1946) Writing and the Alphabet.Cobbett
    Press, London

Nicholls,A. (1983) Managing Educational Innovations.
    George Allen and Unwin,London.
Norman,L.A. (1969) Memory and Attention. John Wiley, New
    York.

Office of the Data Protection Registrar (1985) "The Data
    Protection Act 1984. Guidelines no.1. An introduction
    and Guide to the Act". Office of the Data Protection
    Registrar, Cheshire.

Paisley,W. and Chen,M. (1982) Children and Electronic
    Text: challenges and opportunities of the new
    "literacy". Institute for Communication
    Research,Stanford.
Papert,S. (1980) Mind Storms. Harvester Press, Brighton.
Petrella,R.I.(1984) "Technology and Employment in Europe:
    problems and proofs". Science and Public Policy 11. 6.
    352-9.

Bibliography

Pringle, M.K. (1973) The Roots of Violence and Vandalism. National Children's Bureau, London.

Rooke,D.(1984) "Education: investment in human assets". Paper to the Standing Conference on School Science and Technology, London

Sagan,C. (1977) The Dragons of Eden: speculations on the evolution of human intelligence. Random House, New York.

SCDC.(1984) The School Curriculum Development Committee.SCDC, London.

Shirley,S. (1984) "Social Consequences of the Electronic Revolution". Science and Public Policy 11. 6. 350-1.

Sommerlatte,T.W. (1982) "Strategic Approaches to Office Automation" in International Telecommunications (K.L.Lanchester,ed.) D.C.Hutt, New York

Stibic,V. (1980) Personal Documentation for Professionals.North Holland, Amsterdam.

Stibic,V. (1982) Tools of the Mind: techniques and methods for intellectual work. North Holland Publishing Co. Amsterdam.

Stonier,T. (1983) The Wealth of Information.

Strassmann,P.A.(1985) Information Payoff: the transformation of work in the electronic age. The Free Press, Macmillan, New York.

Taylor,W. (1981) "Educational Research and Development in the United Kingdom". International Reviews of Education. 27. 2. 179-95.

Toffler,A. (1980) The Third Wave. William Morrow, New York

Waugh,N.C. and Norman,D.A. (1965) "Primary Memory" Psychological Review. 72. 89. 92-3.

Whitehead, D.J. (1980) The Dissemination of Educational Innovations in Britain. Hodder and Stoughton, London.

Whitehead,J (1985) Planning the Electronic Office. Croom Helm, London.

Whitehead,J. (1986) Implementing the Electronic Office. Croom Helm, London.

Williams, B.L. (1932) Ancient Writing and its Influence

Williams,F.(1984) "The Communications Revolution Revisited" Science and Public Policy. 11. 6. 338-42.

Winders, R. (1985) "Putting You Through". Times Higher Educational Supplement 28th June 1985.

Yates,F.A. (1960) The Art of Memory. Routledge and Kegan Paul, London.

INDEX

Index